CROWN OF THORNS

Edited By

TRUDI PURDY

First published in Great Britain in 1993 by
ARRIVAL PRESS
3 Wulfric Square, Bretton,
Peterborough, PE3 8RF

All Rights Reserved

Copyright Contributors 1993

Foreword

Crown of Thorns contains poetry written by people from all walks of life. Reverends and Sisters, plumbers, housewives, builders and children. They all have a great faith in God and in what, for them all, is a way of life. They all feel deeply about their faith and this reflects in the poetry. The poems ask questions and give answers. Most contain a message to the reader, they all proclaim the love of God.

I found compiling *Crown of Thorns* an experience that gave me an insight into why people turn to Christianity. With their faith they gain comfort and inspiration. Which, along with deep feeling, shines through in each poem. A light to guide along the path of life.

Finally, I hope that you enjoy *Crown of Thorns* as much as I did. Compiling it was an uplifting experience, an insight into the contemporary Christian life and faith.

Trudi Purdy

Contents

Solitude	D W Williams	1
Christmas Reality	Anne Joyce	2
The Village Church	John Brooman	3
The Book	P R Dainty	4
Easter Day	Dwight Longencker	5
The Chapel at Poppleton	Peter Hatton	6
One Friday	Sue Elkins	7
Compassion	Olive Miller	8
Time and the Gospel	Patricia Batstone	9
Lonely Bluebell	Peter H Herbert	10
The Prison Chaplain	Anthony Lynett	11
Christmas	J Pitts	12
Untitled	Patrick Hobbs	13
Lost and Found	Katie Bolton	14
Rainbow	Jean Owen	15
Just the Job	Barbara Halstead	16
Grafitti	Philip Isherwood	17
The Spirit Is	Philippa Linton	18
On Lowestoft Beach	Patricia Beacock	19
Serving With Gladness	Betty Gearing	20
Sticky Bud	Simon Baynes	21
Christ in Christie	Barbara Lacey	22
By the Cross of Jesus	P Waite	23
At Roger and Julie's House Meeting	David Robert Watchorn	24
How Great He is	G Manning	25
Dropping the 'T'	Connie Voss	26
Christmas Lights	David J C Wheeler	27
Man of all Seasons	Babs Sherwin	28
God The Father	Barbara Green	29
Heartsease	Iris Lines	30
Precious Promises	F E Mullis	31
Needs	C Purden	32
Song of Praise to These I Have Loved	Edna Wright	33

What Nonsense	Joyce Kimpton	35
The Garden	Joyce Robson	36
Easter	Winnie Wright	37
God is Where you Find Him	Len Stephens	38
Easter	R Hall	39
The Christmas Myth?	Kenneth Nicholson	40
The Dilemma	Johnnie Atherton	41
Nevertheless	Constance Grey	42
A Word With God	Ann Wilkinson	43
A Birthday Card	Randle Manwaring	44
Freely Give	Barbara Whittles-Preston	45
Prayer	Mike Smith	46
Christmas Joy	Joyce Wakely	47
How I Feel	E Want	48
Good Friday	Irene W Dulson	49
A Time for Pain	Brenda Benton	50
Synod	Ron Shaddick	51
Eastertime	Kathleen Beale	52
To the Class of '92	Janet Llewellyn	53
Let Go	Barbara Collier	54
Judas Iscariot	Dorothy K Backler	55
The Crib the Cross the Crown	Frances C Akhurst	56
No Lovelier Time	Ted Harben	57
Jesus Speaks Today	Kathleen B Hutchings	58
At Peace	Geoffrey Gostick	59
Life	Marion Houghton	60
To a White Violet	Joy Hedges	61
The Reason Why	Genevieve Grewer	62
The Practice of Prayer	Paul Scott	63
Peace	Sue Richards	64
Jericho Road	Ruth Nickerson	65
Souls Immortal	Joyce Walker	66
Is There Sweet Music?	E Gwendoline Keevill	67
Crossroads	Rachel Evans	68
Untitled	R Shawcroft	69
Nicodemus to the Wind	Muriel Taylor	70
Kneel Before the Cross	Nicola Benn	71

Title	Author	Page
Untitled	Chris Coupe	72
Miracles Happen	A H Shepherd	73
Giving Till it Hurts	Frank Morley	74
Mere Mortal	Liz Knowles	75
Jesus Meets Us	Eric Wyld	76
A Hymn	Audrey J Sizer	77
Belonging	R Kemp	78
Worthy the Lamb	Kathleen Pike	80
Letting Go	Alisoun M Ward	81
Shopping for a God	Linda Smith	82
See Here I Am...	H Collins	83
Pilgrimage	O Burchill	84
A Christmas Rap	Ellen Ralls	85
My Emmaus	Patrick Sherring	86
Gethsemane	Sarah J Honour	87
The Open Door	Nancy Morley	88
The True Vine	Mavis Tebby	89
Candle - Light at Willen	Barbara Clifton	90
Earth Talk, Rio, 1992	Hilary Elfick	91
Peace	F Aspin	92
A Poem for Good Friday	Derek Lawrence	93
Homeless	Sister Jean Oglethorpe	94
For a Pilgrim	George Brigham	95
Comparison	Rosemary Payne	97
Seeing is Believing	Walter Riggans	98
Easy Religion	A B Mossta	99
Untitled	Mary Graves	100
Good Friday Thoughts on Christmas	Aubrey Ridge	101
Praying Time	Rachel J Sparks	102
As a Child	Sheila Winson	103
The Christ of the Burned Men	Tim Marks	104
Church on Sundays	Ann Page	105
Senses	Gerry Brown	106
Corpus Christi	Veronica Faulks	107
Riches	Dorothy Woo	109
Them	Alan Sourbut	110

Pilgrimage	C J E Lefroy	111
Two Bowls of Water	Malcolm Beech	112
Alive	Michael Saward	114
Empathy	Simon Horn	115
Why Me	Tom Luke	116
Scattered Seed	Christine Hope	117
Shine On Jesus	Roy L Barber	118
Temptation	Grace S Edgoose	119
Veronica	Grace Nicholls	120
Confusion	Margaret Godden	121
Blind before Him	Emma Bateman	123
True Joy	E Maisie Clegg	124
Christmas Bells	Mary Anderson	125
The Answer	Mary Peagram	126
The Secret	Marjorie Short	127
The Person on the Poster	Alan Meacock	128
Meditation on Ploughed Earth	Rosamy Murphy	129
Greed	Simon Martin	130
Go Forth	Briony Lill	131
Sunset Reverie	Doris Cole	132
Of Regal Birth	Gerald Gardiner	133
Shedding	Coral Rumble	134
Requiem	Eddy Hughes	135
My Issac?	Connie Webb	136
Maundy Thursday	F G Whitelock	137
Jubilee	Anthony Harper	138
The Daily Battle	Janis Priestley	139
Untitled	Sarah Cope	140
Ponsonby Churchyard in June	R G Head	141
The Robe	Ann Searle	142
The Hill of Life	Marie Pettitt	143
Some Verses from Psalm 104...	Sheila Lloyd	144
Disciple	Sue Hobson	146
Advent	Maggie Doré	147
Lenten Evensong	Mary Atterbury	148
My Soul	Sarah Threadkell	149
I Know There is a God	Christine Algar	150

Jesus	Mary A Foden	152
Manchester City Mirage	David Hardman	153
The Way	M Groves	154
Promises	Hilary Hutchinson	155
Ode to an Innocent	Della Smithson	156
Christmas Thoughts	Derek Hurst	157
Within the Boundaries of Friendship	Caroline Rose	158
The Spirit Comes	Tessa Spanton	159
Moses Reflects	Joe Whittaker	160
We All Have Our Prisons	Peter Zimmermann	161
Time	Evelyn M Deakin	162
Seeing, Yet Not Seeing	Stanley Finch	163
Hope	Marian Bullock	164
Stewards of the Lord's Supper	H Chilton	165
Legacy	Cathie Walton	166
The King's Highway	Geoffrey Lund	167
I Am a Pearl Lord	Heather Connolly	168
The Way Ahead	Peter Swan	169
The Forgotten Friend	Lisa Cornwell	170
If Jesus Came...	Betty Roe	171
Echoes	R A Ruddock	172
Lucy	Jill Edwards	173
Hope	Marjorie Evans	174
Soul Sounds	Kenneth Whittaker	175
Harvest	Linda Davis	176
In Quietness and Confidence Shall Be Your Strength	Freda Head	177
Today is Mine	Joyce Faulkner	178
Seasons of Forgiveness	Richard Keen	179
Silvan	Robin Arnfield	180
Preacher	Andrew Moll	181
Sign Language	Christine Leonard	182
Challenge	Judith Dye	183
Invitation	Valerie Pimperton	185
Gutter Theology	P Longbottom	186
The Need of the Hour	Jean Roberts	187

We Praise You Lord	Penny Brooks	188
Heaven	Christine Woodward	189
A Poem for Good Friday	Trude Bedford	190
The Retired Gardener	Kathleen Stevens	191
The Seekers	D H Cooper	192
Go Forth with Faith	Mary L Ticehurst	193
Advent	Maureen Bedford	194
His Presence	Barbara E Higgins	195
Autumn Leaves	D Parker	196
Genesis	Alfred John Winfield	197

Solitude

There are times when silence is as the fragrance of the rose;
Pure distillation of Eternity; the essence of repose;
Or sometimes as the rainbow hues, the seven-colour span,
Ennobling the peace below; the promised peace to man:
But then it can be dark, as midnight when the moon has gone,
When ravens' wings are blacker still; bereft of glimmers of the sun:
Or maybe turgid, as a syrup sea, that treacles round the mind
And leaves the senses scentless and makes one's thinking blind.
The kind of silence one will know must lie within the brain:
Do you, with fear, hide from storms or uplift your face to rain?
Thus it is with solitude; a heaven or a hell:
How are you to live with? - for it's with you, you must dwell.

D W Williams

Christmas Reality

A sea of scowling faces rushes round the store,
Hassled by the chore in hand, children wanting more.

Joyful Christmas carols are floating on the air,
Trolleys bulge with festive treats, but sadness everywhere.

Inside the plastic grotto the charade of Santa Claus
Is re-enacted yet again, 'It's all in a good cause.'

Sarah knows he isn't real, his beard is cotton wool.
He smells of beer and cigarettes, they must think she's a fool.

At the carol service another tale is told,
Of God born in a stable, she must be getting old!

Sarah can't believe these things, Santa's just a fake,
And so the blessed Christchild will too be a mistake.

But from his thronely splendour a God of love looks on,
And weeps for little Sarah, who won't accept His Son.

The baby of the manger grew up to be a man
Of love, authority and power. He was God's rescue plan.

They stripped him of his clothing, whipped him 'til he bled,
Nailed him to a wooden cross, a thorn crown pierced his head.

Once more weak and helpless, death claimed him on the tree.
Death lost the fight, he came to life, a glorious victory.

Jesus is alive today, not fake like Santa Claus.
He came to be our Saviour. He's mine - will he be yours?

Anne Joyce

The Village Church

The Village Church, of weathered pastel greys,
Oblivious to time and measured days,
Lies nestled where the cottages surround
And dizzy tombstones litter hallowed ground.

Evergreen stand sentinel the yews,
To mark a gravelled path to time-worn pews,
Where learned folk or simpleton or squire,
Would once in time to reverence aspire.

A melancholy aura doth belie,
This sad old heart that beats to sanctify,
For few are those its inner life do share,
And many those who for it little care.

If only shrouded eyes might truly see,
This priceless heritage perchance would be
A stepping stone to resurrection's shore -
A live, pulsating village heart once more.

John Brooman

The Book

I do not love this Book because it is
Black enough to please Puritans,
Holy enough to scare demons,
Thick enough to stop bullets,
Heavy enough to squash flies,
But because sometimes when I read it
I am moved
Deeper than tears.

I do not love this Book because
Men say it is the very Word of God,
And polish every dot and comma
Like golden ornaments in an idolatrous temple,
But because sometimes when I read it
God speaks in a strange tongue
Deeper than words.

I do not love this book because
The passionate preacher beats the truth out of it
With his blunt fist and his sharp ideas,
(For some use the Book to support their opinions,
As others might use it to support their tables),
But because sometimes when I read it
I am disturbed by a Truth
Deeper than thought.

P R Dainty

Easter Day

It was the grey sky
spread like an old sheet above the green
which, in a grim way,
made the garden cold
and made the spring seem
like an awful thing.

The magnolia blooms
lay heavy and white
on the ground
like slabs of flesh
or pieces of bread.

The wallflowers in
their beds were mottled
in burgundy and
red like dried blood
surrounding open wounds.

The heaviness stayed
for what seemed days;
until for one moment
the sun burned through.
Then the blooms shone white,
the flowers were aflame,
and a small bird sang,
'The garden is new,
the garden is new!'

Dwight Longenecker

The Chapel at Poppleton

Wood grained and dark; a shabby pulpit fall;
Against the leaded lights the chrysallis-born,
Flutter their battered brightness, as the small
Words resound as if they could suborn
This veteran regiment of obedient blocks.
The varnished door, (as the closed window), mocks
The shining winglets frenzied beating,
Till dulled and rent, by the heating
Down they fall. How is it then,
That the next Spring they'll rise again,
To urge another argument than that
Propounded by their dusty habitat?
Are those bright things entombed, or do they breed?
Will they emerge, dishevelled, lost, but freed?

Peter Hatton

One Friday

It used to be so ordinary.
There was nothing special about me:
a London woman child, half-asleep
on a bus marooned in a late-for-work
Friday-morning traffic-jam; when it happened.

> There was nothing special about me.
> I enjoyed Starsky and Hutch on television,
> and evenings in wine bars,
> and pulling on my tight blue jeans
> to shop in Oxford Street on Saturday mornings.

>> And I knew
>> that the after-dark confusion
>> of hands and arms and legs and bitter sweet pain
>> was just the price that must be paid
>> for a man's love.

And I understood,
as I sat typing, that private calls made on the office 'phone
and ballpoints carelessly carried home,
were perks of the job, and I was expected to take them.
And I could expect nothing more.

> And since that Friday?
> Well, I still like television detectives,
> evenings with friends,
> and Saturday mornings shopping.
> But some things have changed -

>> you see, I heard
>> that one Friday
>> a Man loved me enough
>> to die for me.

Sue Elkins

Compassion

When down the path of Youth I trod
Conscience clear and near to God,
Everything was black or white,
I shunned the wrong and loved the right.

Then losing pace a little bit,
I watched how other folks were hit,
How some through no fault of their own
Were sad, neglected, all alone.

And so I stayed to help a while,
To see if I could raise a smile,
Along the way my hands were soiled,
My youthful dreams were all bespoiled.

At last I rested by the way,
Tired but finding time to pray,
Once He had seemed so close and near,
I shed a disillusioned tear.

Then suddenly, like warm, sweet air
I felt His presence everywhere,
No need to search in vain for God,
He walks with us the common sod.

Olive Miller

Time and the Gospel

Time was
        when angels came with news
        and roused unwilling workers from their rest
        to send them to a stable.
        Not too impressed
        they nonetheless obeyed the call
        and found a tiny infant in a stall.
Such times are passed.

Time is
        when leaders call for aid
        and wean uncertain hands to pockets deep
        to bring relief to hungry lands.
        How can we easy sleep
        while distant voices ply their rending pleas,
        discordant as we eat by our TV's?
Such times are now.

Time comes
        when God will call new voices to His cause,
        modern prophets with a message for the world.
        And some will hear, and others pause
        to ask, 'What shall *I* do
        to lead Your wandering people back to You?'
Such times do come.

Patricia Batstone

Lonely Bluebell

Where the leaf furled out from bud,
greening beautifully!
leaning down to touch me, finger -
tip to tip of leaf,
I earthed with God!

Down below a lonely 'bell
chiming dutifully!
blue in prime but quite alone in,
bright but empty, lost
in solitude.

Are you then predestined too,
gentle solitary!
to stand alone outside the crowd?
lonely bluebell, earth
with God through me!

Peter H Herbert

The Prison Chaplain

A passion he had for people,
Expressed in words that few embraced,
And in symbols mysterious and strange
Conjuring no magic for them.

Really he was of no earthly use at all,
And yet there was a fondness which secured his place amidst
The furniture of their minds.

The Gothic script above his door
Spoke volumes.
He had often felt wrong footed
Like a coal fire burning in Summer,
Stoked and fanned,
Ready.
Seldom needed,
In truth seldom wanted.

Faint embarrassment preceded his every arrival,
As though he might dwell on uneasy things,
Like a senile old fool forgetful of propriety.
And he knew their complicity as they
contrived their conversations preserving his naivety,
Like an antique cared for, but never used,
Lest it should crumble under the weight of human flesh.

Anthony Lynett

Christmas

Long nights pursue the shortened days;
Season of sombre, dreary skies,
Symbolic of the world's demise,
Now riven with our roundelays.

Our stencil-patterned lives take wing,
Refreshed with common thoughts of joy,
Displayed in trinket, costly toy
And parcels tied with tinselled string.

Do these proclaim the great event,
Or are we swamped with bogus glee,
Seductive advert, festooned tree
And insulated sentiment?

Now sound the depth of our goodwill:
Ascendent star is topped by time,
The Christ Child birth nailed down in rhyme
And all the lonely lonelier still!

Awake to truth of Christmas-tide!
This child has burst the temporal chain,
Receiving hearts have naught but gain,
And life's horizons open wide.

Take notice of the still small voice,
Take notice of the angels' song,
Our lives, new-born, to Him belong.
Rejoice! Rejoice! Rejoice! Rejoice!

J Pitts

Untitled

Where the trees ache -
the long night listening,
some-one like a friend will come
easy over the water
to slip a hand between yoke and shoulder,
lift my eyes to the quiet hills,
soft walk with me the morning,
and under hanging skies
I will lay me down
like leaf to warm earth falling.

Patrick Hobbs

Lost and Found

You reached out your hand
To touch my face,
But I turned my head away.
I heard your voice
Calling my name,
But I closed my ears to the noise.
You waited patiently
For so long,
With your arms open wide,
Ready to hold me,
But I did not want your love.
I wanted to be alone,
To proudly say
That I did not need your help.
Mercifully your wisdom
Is greater than my foolishness,
Your love,
Much deeper than my hate.
You called me again
And this time I heard.
I gathered up my shattered self,
And thankfully made my way home.

Katie Bolton

Rainbow

Lord God whose promises are never broken.
A covenant You made with man,
That never more would You destroy him.
A bow of colour sealed the plan.
You split the light with sun and shadow,
Scattered it through drops of rain,
That all may see Your glory scattered,
Find a rainbow in the pain.
A sight so wonderful to see,
From light and water, spilt for me.
Jesus came, His glory hidden,
Sent by You as human too,
It was only by His killing
That the rainbow light shone through.
His broken light shone forth in brilliance
On the day He rose anew.
The beauty of our risen Saviour
Showed God's promise had come true.
The rainbow split and separated,
Sent through all the world abroad
Will be strongest when united
In the temple of the Lord.
The whole kaleidoscope of colour
Worshipping, the Christ our God.

Jean Owen

Just the Job

'I was only doing the job I'm paid to do.'
So the soldier said who marched Him up the Hill,
Towards the place of execution.
'I was only doing the job I was forced
To do,' so said the man called Simon,
Conscripted into carrying the cross-beam that
The prisoner, Jesus, was too weak to bear.
(He'd been thrashed and whipped before
Ever His last long slow journey had begun.)
'I was only doing the work that any carpenter
Might have to do,' said one who had to hammer
In the nails to hold His body on the gibbet in the air.
'We were only doing the job we're called upon to do,
Upholding Jewish Law, and supporting that tradition
Which says God won't choose new untested ways
To show His power.' So said the leaders of the nation
Who had cheated, bribed, and fixed His trial to get
A guilty verdict, and they jeered at Jesus hanging on the Tree.

And Jesus looked with kindness as He saw a soldier,
Tired and worn after a heavy tour of duty.
He smiled His thanks at the sad black face of strong,
Kind Simon of Cyrene, and to the carpenter His look of
understanding said, 'I, too, know what it's like
To be glad to take a job, any job with wood.'
And the sadness on His face, when the Priests and Lawyers
Hurled abuse, showed love - still - even for them,
His enemies and murderers.
What could a man, a God, like Him be doing dying there?
Surely it was all a bad mistake? But, 'No, I'm here,' Jesus our
Saviour said, 'Just doing the job I came to do.'

Barbara Halstead

Grafitti

The scrawled rebellion to pain
kept on the walls inside our hearts;
kept as a permanent stain
to reflect upon,
with pain
or anger.
Perhaps we don't realise
others can only see the mess.

I think God has a
great healing wall,
big enough to take
all our grafitti;
healing that changes
the words and the meaning
to see, eventually,
something beautiful.

If I stop writing on my own walls,
perhaps they will disappear.

Philip Isherwood

The Spirit Is

White bird in circling
the sweet dove descending
brush my soul with your grace
I soar into your peace

Wild wind in the forest
oh trees in the trembling
shake my heart in your power
I sing in the storm

Fierce flame of the Father
pure love of the Saviour
baptise me with fire
my heart is your ember

The caress and the hunting
the silence, the grandeur
the dance and the wrestling
the wind and the fire

The Spirit is breaking
earth's barricades open

Philippa Linton

On Lowestoft Beach

To what shall I liken the glory of the Lord?
To the morning sun glittering on the restless sea,
Transforming grey-brown waters into light,
A dazzling path of joyousness for his feet.
Thus is the glory of the Lord.

To what shall I liken the mercy of the Lord?
To the waves rolling over and over on the sand,
Cleaning away the dirt and debris,
Gently obliterating the confused imprints of the past.
Thus is the mercy of the Lord.

To what shall I liken the love of the Lord?
To the endless ocean, cradling the trusting sea-bird,
Safely carrying her in the blustering winds,
An ocean whose depths she does not comprehend.
Thus is the love of the Lord.

Patricia Beacock

Serving With Gladness

When life is sweet and all is serene,
And my skies are a cloudless blue.
The little lambs gambol in fields of green,
And there's nothing obstructing my view.
The pure fresh air in the early morn,
The peace of the countryside,
And I can hear the song of a joyful thrush
As he sings to his new found bride!
When the going is smooth, it is easy my Lord,
To praise you with songs and with rhymes.
To serve you with gladness and joy in my heart,
And to thank you for such happy times!

But when life takes a tumble and nothing goes right,
And those skies turn from blue to grey.
And I can't see the lambs or the fields anymore,
My burdens just get in the way!
The fresh morning air becomes heavy with storms,
And the peace of the countryside broken.
I can no longer hear the song of my thrush,
The end of his story - unspoken.
When the going is rough - it's not easy my Lord,
But with your strength and power and love,
I'll serve you with gladness and joy in my heart,
'Til I join you in heaven above!

Betty Gearing

Sticky Bud

Each February in the dark
and waiting days I take
justified by faith a branch
from the churchyard chestnut tree
and ceremonially break
a twig of life, black treacle buds
long unregarded waiting there
for me.

Be patient
there in its still vase
it preaches, little seen
till life and March and everything
silence my little faith, and leaves
like wings, ceremonially break
from bright shards, and
silently singing
affirm the universe.

Simon Baynes

Christ in Christie

To hear them talk of Genesis you'd think
God capable of but one week.
All done - full stop.
Creation is about our making now
Is in the present tense or not at all;
Our making not
Handfuls of billion years ago but now,
Hourly, minutely, momently;
In detail, minutely, like the insects,
Millions of species of them. God, so many?
Is it because you love them more than us?
Insects? We can't believe it.
Surely we only, we alone with souls,
Sole species of humanity, surely we are
Your greatest love?

There comes no certain answer,
Nothing for proof, nothing that would stand up
In courts of law.
God the detective novelist
Leaves clues throughout the universe -
But is withholding from the publisher
The final chapter.

(Though some of us will swear
We've seen a dog-eared copy of the draft).

Barbara Lacey

By the Cross of Jesus
There stood by the Cross of Jesus - His Mother -
And there was a darkness all over the land.

O blessed darkness come, and shield my dear
From the fierce sun that beats upon His face -
That dries His mouth, and pierces thro' the lids
Of His closed eyes - oh cool His tortured brow!
So high He hangs I cannot reach Him now,
To tend with gentle love His every need.

O blessed darkness come and hide His hands.
I cannot bear to see those bleeding wounds
In hands that once were little, clasped in mine -
Or see His twisted feet, that once would trot
Light-hearted on the path to Nazareth.

O blessed darkness, fall in heavy folds
Between these passing mockers and my son.
They shall not look upon His naked flesh,
And taunt Him with His immobility -
He is my Son! The Son of God most high!
They shall not look upon His agony.

O blessed darkness come, and like a shroud
Wrap round the body of my dying Son,
As once I wrapped Him in His swaddling bands,
And held Him ever safely in my arms -
'Twill not be long - oh dark grow deeper yet.

Grow deeper yet, and hide my falling tears;
I will not let Him see my agony -
I feel it all - the thorns, the nails, the spear -
My heart bursts open with His suffering!
O come thou blessed darkness, swiftly come -
From burning torment, bring my dear release.
P Waite

At Roger and Julie's House Meeting

A more Christian couple quite hard to find
Thoughtful, caring, genuinely kind,
Opening their home to all who care
To join their fellowship and become aware
Of the power of goodness in this life
Which touches our hearts and ends the strife -
The message of Christ - whom they have heard
Now called by him to spread His word.
So thank you Lord, for allowing us near
Your Holy Spirit, as we sit here,
For all I know, when I leave this place,
Is my mind knows peace, and my heart
feels grace.

David Robert Watchorn

How Great He is

As I gaze at the trees
all beauty and grace
From the Father creator
to the whole human race

I realise, the greatness
The vastness of all
Then problems of life, seem
in comparison, small

Our Father, upon whom we rely
In childlike faith, simple too,
Spans the whole world
with panoramic view

He looks beyond the problems
selects the silver and gold
and weaves the tapestry
as He did in days of old.

He's not confined to field or glen
Cathedral, town or home
The promise of His presence to
us all, where ere we roam.

He sent His son our saviour
To save us from our sin
He came in all humility
Yet now is King of Kings

Jesus crucified upon some wood
a cross so hard to bear
yet rose triumphant from the tomb
Good news for all to share.
G Manning

Dropping the 'T'

'I can't,' my little daughter said
When told she had to make her bed.
'I can't, not now!' my husband cried
When asked to take the bin outside.

My son, when asked to mend a shelf
Said: 'I can't do that.' So I did it myself.
On thinking back it seemed to me
They all forgot how to drop the *t*.

That little word *can't* is so easy, it's true,
When faced with a job we don't want to do.
Oh Lord, if You need us then help us to see
That in serving You we must drop the *t*.

Connie Voss

Christmas Lights

Christmas lights adorn the lamposts,
Tinsel glitters, *Santas* nod,
Wet and glistening are the pavements
Where the weary shoppers plod,
High the prices, cheap the pleasure,
Noisy tills and traffic's hum,
Can you hear, above the bustle,
Angel voices - 'Christ will come!'

Christmas lights upon the lamposts
Pain and joy see, both a rod,
Wet and glistening is the pavement
That the prostitute just trod,
Pubs are full, they call it *leisure*,
But it is their life to some,
Listen, through the glasses' clatter,
Angel voices - 'Christ will come!'

Christmas lights glow on the lamposts
As the sky with dawn is shod,
White with snow, the glistening pavement
Speaks the purity of God,
Sleep lies on the silent city,
Last night's fun was but a crumb,
Hear a new sound, sweet, triumphant,
Angel voices - 'Christ *is* come!'

David J C Wheeler

Man of all Seasons

Born a King at Winter time
Raised a child at Summer
Became a man at Autumn tide
And died for us at Spring

A Babe, a King, born in the cold
Came to fulfil, the prophets of old
One would be born to a Virgin mild
Mary His Mother, Jesus her child

A child running free, in warm Summer sun
Did He but know, He was the Chosen One
Listening to priests, quiet as a mouse
Learning the law, in His Father's House

Thirty years old, with leaves turning brown
He and His twelve preached in each town
Walking on the water, raising Lazarus up
Too soon it would be time for deaths bitter cup

Blossom upon each bough of the tree
Flowers opening wide, Spring's sun to see
A Man on a cross, the cross towering high
Arms wide, outstretched, ready to die

A Man of all Seasons, Jesus our Friend
At one with Nature, right to the end

Babs Sherwin

God The Father

No adjective can aptly show the greatness of our God:
Giver of Life; Creator,
Giver of Grace, Redeemer.
The mind can scarcely comprehend the greatness
                              of our God;
He is Infinity.

And yet we feel His presence, and we know that
                              He is there -
His spirit is within us,
To counsel and to cheer us -
We can call on Him in trouble; we can look to
                              Him in joy;
Accepting love and care.

No adjective can aptly show the greatness of our God:
But Jesus came to tell us,
His precious son has taught us
We have a Heavenly Father,
And He is ever near.

So, Holy Spirit, help us, as we turn to
                        God the Father
With an ever present problem, or a doubt that
                              comes our way -
'He understands!' the preacher told us,
                    and we turn to you, dear Father:
'Please help us, Lord; forgive us;'
And this is how we pray.

Barbara Green

Heartsease

Walk in the garden and feel God is there.
His handiwork lifts the heart in prayer.
Uplifted by the scented breeze,
A burdened soul finds quiet ease.
And in the sweet and restful calm,
Comes the comforting, healing, balm
When the sun beats down, there's apple tree shade,
But leaves must fall and petals fade.
Rain streams down, and strong wind blows,
So, the peace of the garden goes.
Then - a robin sings with all his might.
The buds are only tucked out of sight.
They will need a season of rain,
To make the garden bloom again.
So, God warms the heart through Winter's chill,
And He's always there, through good and ill.
Summer and Winter, His love is the same,
When hearts are lifted in His precious Name.

Iris Lines

Precious Promises

Change my heart O God,
That I may catch and hold,
The pure scintillating beauty
behind the streams of gold,
That flows from myriads of stars,
That grow surely and slowly dim.
As I wait with bated breath,
To catch a glimpse of Him.
I gaze upon your sweeping train
Of brilliant azure blue,
Turning mountains and streams that sparkle
Into facets of every hue.
Let me be still, and drink in
The beauty of each blessed morn.
To taste the Spirit of Life,
That refreshes and bathes the golden dawn
And I wait to hear the trumpet proclaim
His expectant return to earth.
Darkness disappears and I rejoice
At His Promise of the World's New Birth.

F E Mullis

Needs

What worth our lives if paths were ever straight,
If fortune always smiled upon our way.
If flowers were aye in bloom and ne'er a thorn
Would there be need of trust, or need to pray?

What worth our minds if thoughts were ever simple,
No time at crossroads when we must decide,
If every step were easy on the journey
Would there be need of friend, or need of guide?

What worth our hearts if they had not felt sorrow,
If ever laughter filled, nor known a tear,
But ever quiet, peaceful and contented,
Would there be need of strength or need of cheer?

What worth our faith if it were never tested,
To prove in time of trial it is true,
And show that it can rise, unchanged, o'er sadness
Would you have need of God - or He of you?

C Purden

Song of Praise to These I Have Loved

Whenever I see the sunset glow
Aflame in the evening sky
My heart is filled with a song of praise
To the Glory of God on High

Whenever I see our old grey Church
Steadfast and calm as a nun
My Soul is filled with the peace of God
And His dearly beloved Son

Whenever I see a tiny babe
held close to a mother's heart
I think of the Christ Child's tender love
Of which we are all a part

Whenever I see the trees in spring
Young and Graceful and green.
I think of the glorious Easter morn
And the triumph of Christ supreme

Whenever I see the birds in flight
And hear their songs of praise
I think of the souls in the Father's care
And the Joy of eternal days.

Whenever my sweet cat looks at me
With his sea green eyes of love
Thanks be to God for these little ones
Placed in our care from above.

Whenever I see a field of corn
Rippling, golden and fair
I think of the manifold love and gifts
He has given us all to share.

Whenever I see a tiny boy
With hair of fine spun gold
I think of my own dear darling son
And the wonderful gift we hold.

Whenever I see the roseate hue
Of the early May day dawn
I think of a dark haired baby girl
And the joy when she was born.

Whenever I see my loved ones kneel
At Christ's own feet in prayer
I offer my hearts deep thankfulness
To the Father who led them there.

Edna Wright

What Nonsense

There's nothing like nonsense for making you think.
It gives you a shock and you suddenly blink -
Did my hearing deceive me, did somebody wink?
She's normally sane and not given to drink?
I know it means something, I'll just have to think.

When the tyrant was bored he would send for the Fool,
The man who was licensed to mock at his rule
When everyone else was his terrified tool.
He's comic and yet it reminds him of school -
But no need to be angry, it's only the Fool!

What nonsensical notions the Master did preach
Like the camel and needle, the better to breach
The conservative concepts of those he would teach -
And it always meant more than a figure of speech.
He needed the nonsense, it helped him to preach!

Well, I looked for a moral and all I could find
Was the notion that Truth is too big for my mind.
I can't comprehend it, just can't take it in
(Maybe something to do with Original Sin).
Think of Predestination opposed to Free-will
And all the philosophers arguing still!
When the first shall be last and the last shall be first
And salvation comes not to the best but the worst,
The paradox simply takes off and you find
It leaves reason and common-sense limping behind.

Maybe nonsense is one of God's signposts to say
'If you throw all your preconceived notions away
I will give you My Truth at the end of the day.'

Joyce Kimpton

The Garden

It may have been the first time,
The lovely willow wept,
To see Our Lord and Saviour - alone,
While the disciples slept.
The flowers in the garden,
Must have hung their heads down low,
How could they bear to see the pain,
Of Him who loved them so.
The birds would sing their sweetest song,
To soothe His aching heart,
I'm sure that all of nature,
Tried hard to play its part.
But only God the Father,
Could give the healing balm,
Could speak the words He needed,
To make Him cool and calm.
With God around - inside Him,
He was complete and whole,
The world may bruise His body,
But it couldn't touch His soul.
Dear Lord - may we be given,
A faith so strong and true,
No matter what may come to us,
We'll know we're loved by You.

Joyce Robson

Easter

At Easter many years ago
A man was crucified
He became a man for our sakes
And for our sakes He died

This Holy man was innocent
Of the charges which were laid
His only fault was to love all men
So for love His life He gave.

The cross was large and heavy
With nails through hands and feet
A crown of thorns upon His head
The dreadful wounds were deep.

They spat upon His tired face
Mocking 'King of the Jews,' they said
For men were ever cruel
Whilst down His blood ran red.

At last it is finished was His cry
The agony, humility and pain
Jesus our Saviour who died for all
Hung crucified in the rain.

It was not the end for Christ arose
On the third day praise His name
Now in our world He lives and loves
The Saviour forever, and ever the same.

Winnie Wright

God is Where you Find Him

In a large hospital ward
A tired doctor at a bedside
Listens, attentive and sympathetic.
Then he gently explains the treatment with care,
And God smiles up at him as He lies there.

A couple, reconciled,
And mutually forgiving,
Tenderly embrace and start anew,
And the arms of God are round those two.

A widow, grieving for the one she has lost,
Pours out her pain and guilt
To the kindly listener at her side,
Easing the expression of her grief.
And God is there, too, holding her hand,
And lovingly bringing relief.

A nurse picks up a starving child,
She holds him tenderly to her
All skin and bones and large head
Covered with sores and dirt.
His eyes stare, ringed with flies,
And tears of compassion fill God's eyes.

Len Stephens

Easter

As the faithful women sought Him
Ere the dawning of the day,
As they came on feet of sorrow
To find the great stone rolled away;

As they came with oil of mourning
To pay homage to their dead,
And were startled with the message
Of a risen Lord instead;

As Mary, in the garden, weeping,
Wrapped in sorrow for her Lord -
Recognising not her Master,
Till He spoke that gentle word -

Spoke her name, in tone familiar;
Joy of joys! Her heart awakes -
Leaps in gladness to adore Him,
Ere her homeward way she takes.

So may we, with hearts rejoicing,
Share the victory of Thy Cross,
Freed from sin by Thine atonement,
Counting every gift but loss -

If this day of Resurrection
Finds no response within our heart,
if it leaves us, still uncaring,
Unready yet to take our part.

O my Saviour and Redeemer,
So involved our souls to free,
May our hearts be Thine completely,
To serve and worship only Thee.
R Hall

The Christmas Myth?

They said the Christmas story was a myth that wasn't true.
The Virgin Birth was fantasy - as everybody knew!
The evidence for three wise men was very, very frail,
And the story of the shepherds just a naive fairy tale!
And long before the era when BC became AD,
Men told of gods who left their heavens, and donned humanity.
So there's nothing very special about Jesus and his birth;
It's just another legend of a god who came to earth!

But are these stories simply myths? Please help me, Lord, to see
The truth that underlies the fact of Christ's nativity.
That God should abdicate his throne in heaven, and come to earth,
Is a far greater miracle than any virgin birth.
I'm glad those simple shepherds were the first on earth to hear
The heavenly choir proclaiming that the King of Heaven was here!
They came to pay their homage to the new-born baby King,
They came to bring their love, because they'd nothing else to bring.

I don't know who those Magi were who travelled from afar;
There's no way I can prove there ever was a guiding star;
Nor can I prove that love exists, that Summer follows Spring;
But faith affirms these stories have an honest, truthful ring;
So let me join those shepherds, and the wise men from the East,
The poor man, and the rich man, from the greatest to the least;
They brought their gifts, appropriate to peasant or to king.
How can my gift be worthy, if it's less than everything!

Kenneth Nicholson

The Dilemma

Where is there peace
For the loving mind?
Each new desire
And heart of fire
Grows cold upon reflection,
That what was new
Is shortly due
To cease.

Where goes the ideal
Of eternal love?
Each *ever and ever*
Ties never sever
Grow cold with rejection,
And what was dear
Is very near
Ordeal.

Why does the heart
Recover once more
To have again
That moment when,
It warms with affection
And once again
You never deign
To part.

Johnnie Atherton

Nevertheless

The clouds are scudding fast across the sky,
a Summer gale is blowing through my trees
which bow and bend beneath the mighty breeze.
It's warm enough to sit outside,
enjoy the wind about my head and face -
the wind that brings nostalgic pictures
of green clad hills with purple peaks,
of walking shoes, a stick, a scarf,
days which for me are past and gone.
No, it is not old age which holds me here
but rigidity and pain which has not yet a cure,
which one day in God's mercy will be revealed
to men of skill and science.
A rest, enforced, has many compensations -
this rustling, roaring wind has much to say.
Is not God's Holy Spirit likened to a wind,
enabling great things?
For some the power comes to speak and preach,
to go for God to distant lands;
to demonstrate for justice and for right
in a selfish, stricken world.
For others of us, may it be
a strength to face whatever comes?
A listening ear, a readiness to share
our experience of God's love and care?

Constance Gray

A Word With God

Dear Father God, again we come
In loving memory of your son.
He gave his life that we might know
Your love for us on earth below.

He showed us how you love us all
Despite our sin, whene'er we fall.
Never will your love reject us;
Your Spirit always will protect us.

Bless us with all the things we need,
Fill us with love, inspire each deed.
Forgive us for the wrongs we've done;
Help us to live as did your son.

In your good time may we all be
Dear Father, Spirit, Son, with Thee
When wars will end, and conflicts cease
Where reigns for ever perfect peace.

Ann Wilkinson

A Birthday Card

Thinking and reading and scribbling,
poetry has been a way of life;
in people and places everywhere
there has often been a poem.

Sometimes a whisper in my ear
turns a pumpkin into a coach,
whilst from the treasury of living
much loveliness arises.

I believe in belief, I believe in love,
strong in the texture of creation,
despite the many tragedies
none can fully explain.

I have loved life and seen good days,
therefore I give the fullest praise
to my Creator, Sustainer, Redeemer,
weaving my eighty years.

Randle Manwaring

Freely Give

I cannot reach, see, or feel,
Chased by clouds of darkest night;
Mindful, fearing, torn apart,
'Why me?' I cried, with trembling heart.

This day, with courage healed, I turn,
look back across the passing night,
Knowing it did bring to me
God's glorious, powerful, healing light.

My heart is filled with hope anew,
Gone the doubt and fear.
All part of mine His hand has blessed;
I know now always He is near.

The heavens, earth and waters deep,
The beast that walks, the bird in flight;
To His works I give my all,
I freely give the Lord my life.

Barbara Whittles-Preston

Prayer

My prayer for us all as we pause to pray
Is that we think of each other every day
And that we will not stop or wait
If we hear of one in need
To go and freely do for them
A loving Christian deed.

Let us start and forever continue
To think of one another
As our nearest and our dearest
Sister and brother.

For we will never enter Heaven's door
If we do not help those who are poor.
Those who need clothes, warmth and food
Are all members of God's brotherhood.

Let us go to help the lame and blind
The sick in body, spirit and mind.
May we visit the lonely every day
And then we can together pray.

For when we meet as two or more
Jesus tells us we can be sure
He'll be there with us as we pray
And remain as we go on our way.

So with God's own son helping you and me
May our motto from this day on be:
You need no longer pray alone
For we will come to comfort thee.

Mike Smith

Christmas Joy

Traitors to the truth we cheat and
Glamorise the Christmas story.
Tinsel, plastic baubles cannot
Serve to dim our Lord's true glory.
In the midst of man's despairing
Came a God who showed His caring.

God incarnate, born of Mary
In a strange, unfriendly city.
Born a Baby weak and helpless
In a world of little pity.
Can we show what Christmas Joy means
On a card with pretty snow-scenes?

Fancy parcels, cheeky robins,
Ribbons, wreaths for decoration,
Cannot hide the pain and anguish
Of our God's humiliation.
Fleeing from a mad King's fury;
Banished from His place in Jewry.

Into manhood still He suffered.
Stayed with outcasts, shared their sadness.
Healed the sick, forgave the sinner -
Orthodoxy called it madness!
'Til the evil power that claimed them
Tried to kill the love that shamed them.

Come then, celebrate this wonder!
God with grace and mercy meets us
As responding to His loving
We are saved from what defeats us.
Christmas holds this deeper reason
For rejoicing at this season.
Joyce Wakely

How I Feel

The *power* of His Spirit is now working in me
I must not contain it, for others must see
My heart burns within me; in a very strange way.
I know it is God, He's having His way.

The *joy* of His Spirit is flooding my soul
Giving me peace and making me whole
Filling my heart right up to the brim
My cup runneth over with love for Him.

This *power* and this *joy* He's given to me
You too can have it: the offer is free
And peace in my heart; which the world cannot give
I know it is mine for as long as I live.

E Want

Good Friday

The sky darkened, thunder rolled
From the hour of noon till three,
That day they killed our Saviour
On the Cross, to make us free.

Crowds had gathered round to jeer
As fiercely they dragged Him by
To the Hill of Calvary -
Where they hung Him up to die.

From the Cross He gazed on friends
Who were with the throng that day,
His Mother was there with them -
Just a little space away.

As the murderers offered gall
He cried out with startling sound
'Forgive them all, dear Father,'
He died, darkness fell around.

The earth shook - in the temple
The blest veil was rent in two!
No sun shone. All awed, cried out
'He's died for us - it's true.'

Often our lives are darkened o'er
We say to friends 'Is God here?'
Keep praying, take heart again
We'll find that God is near.

For He's our Rock, strength, and shield -
Just a breath, a sigh away.
When we've found a love like His
From such love, how can we stray?
Irene W Dulson

A Time for Pain

The agony of Christ is real
so real to me that I can feel.
Each nail as it pierces His skin
in a battle only He could win.
I share His pain, so hard to bear,
by trusting I am in His care.

The darkness is now drawing nigh
and to His Father He does cry.
'Father why have You forsaken me?'
But this is the way it has to be.
So many times I've cried out too,
when I've not known what I must do.

This is the price we have to pay
when we walk Christ's righteous way.
The way is hard, the road is steep,
and into darkness we must leap.
Then He will take us by the hand
and guide us to the promised land.

Brenda Benton

Synod

Words bounce off the wall
Like balls on a squash court
But this is no game
The serious business of the Church
Has to be attended to.

Here there are implications for
Young and old, men and women,
Saint and sinner and those delicate
Relations with other Churches.
Here a darkness can infiltrate the mind.

Yet, now and again, shafts of insight
With needle sharpness
Pierce the darkness and bring
New hope and substance to the Agenda.

What would Moses have made of it?
Or old Elijah or Jeremiah?
Would St Paul have approved?
Would echoes of Sinai, Carmel
Or Mars Hill direct their thinking?

Above all, it must be asked,
Would Jesus approve?
Just to enquire
Is something.

Ron Shaddick

Eastertime

So much to learn from life's long journey
Of beauty, truth; of pain and loss
The love of friends, of husband, children
The radiant mystery of Christ's Cross
Revealing, as the years go by
His love, which will not, cannot die

What peace, what joy, his presence gives
Through all the lonely, quiet hours
To know the loved ones now in Heaven
Live on, in joy with new found powers
Their free and active spirits
Touching these lives of ours
In heart and mind, they are often near
To comfort, understand, and cheer
Still one in spirit, as of yore
His agents still, the wide world o'er

And in the garden, nature too, bestirs herself
With joy, responding to the warm sun
And rain and gentle breeze
To dress herself in beauty, colour,
fragrance, all contending
To give our earthly home a wondrous peace

How foolish not to choose our Father's way
Wherein his guiding, cleansing power
Always forgiving, leads us on
Renewed, with strength for every hour

Kathleen Beale

To the Class of '92

Jesus told them of the secret that now belonged to them,
the secret of the kingdom, where God would dwell with men.

He said 'Those on the outside are the ones who don't draw near.
God's Word to man is close at hand, and those with ears may hear.'

'Many come to look and see, yet their minds do not perceive
their spiritual desolation and the healing that they need.'

'I use parables and paradox, words to make men think,
they listen, but never understand and assume there is no link.'

'Otherwise these people might, see the sin that holds them fast,
hear of God's free forgiveness, and turn back to him at last.'

Christian always use your eyes and in your mind perceive
the God beyond the tangible, and in your heart believe.

Christian use your ears to hear and prayer to understand
the whisper of His Spirit, for your King is close at hand.

Christian always use the throne, for grace is freely given
to those who turn back day by day, in trust, to God in heaven.

Janet Llewellyn

Let Go

Let go my child.
Do not be afraid to fall into my hands -
The hands of the living God.
I will not crush you, but support you.
I have been waiting so long
To take you in my arms,
But you would not let go.

Your fingers were twined so tightly
Around that Something.
You thought you needed it,
That it would help you,
But it let you down.
And now you have nothing
And no-one left to cling to
But Me.

I have been here all the time,
But you could not see Me or hear Me
When I tried to speak to you -
So busy you were and burdened.

Rest now,
Here in the secret place of My shadow.
It will not be dark for long.
Soon the brightness of My Glory
Will dazzle you.
You will be quickened and revived as never before.
Not that you may leap up and rush
Out of My Presence,
But that you may walk forth with Me
In newness of life.

Barbara Collier

Judas Iscariot

Oh no, my friend, it wasn't the price of the ointment,
Or the thirty pieces of silver - I held the bag, after all.
He could have quenched mere greed with one of His glances
Or His voice, as He told a tale that spoke to the soul.
I wanted a King, a leader who'd fight for his country,
The spear, bloodshed and hatred and power;
Crushing the tyrants who scorned and tormented our people,
His persistent patience made my heart turn sour:
So I sought His death. He knew it, but would not deter me,
Accepted the kiss which ensured His capture and pain;
Called me friend, that others might not construe it
An act of betrayal - hiding my guilt once again.
But the silver that bought His life is not gain to me,
My life shall end, like His whom I sold, on a tree.

Dorothy K Blackler

The Crib the Cross the Crown

Uncomprehending, the man, back bent against the wind
Spurs on the beast.
Time, so little time.
Unseeing, unafraid -
The girl this night has angel thoughts.
Not here, no room
But Heaven decrees a place is found
A wail, the little Child
This Love, our God Himself enshrines.
Above His head a cross of holy light

A holy light, rending the gloom and dark of earth
With piercing ray.
Time, so little time.
For men would dark prefer
And by their evil ways the light destroy.
Not here, no room
They clamour now, away with Him.
O Love, O Holy One
O Word of God. Men knew Him not
The world's great Light. Has God forsaken now?

Forsaken now? The Lord of life in anguish cries
'Father forgive
Now, for endless time.'
The fearful cross, the tomb
His broken body hold, and darkness reigns.
Arise! Shine forth!
Thy light is come, the way of love
From earth to highest heaven
Is radiant now, to man revealed.
Salvation comes, our Lord, our King is crowned.

Frances C Akhurst

No Lovelier Time

No lovelier time on earth than this,
Joy mantles all with heavenly bliss,
The world erupts and sings;
And men like children, starry-eyed,
Dream of the dawn of Christmas-tide,
Of home, and golden things.

Who has not felt since life began
Some stirring for this Son of Man
Born of so pure a maid?
When carols thrill with telling mirth
Strange message of mysterious birth,
Who has not sensed the right of things
In lowly shepherds, stately kings,
And baby - manger laid?

No happier time on earth is known,
Seeds of goodwill are freely sown,
And peace - a haven finds;
When men and women on one glad day,
For purer hearts are moved to pray,
And nobler, Christ-like minds.

Ted Harben

Jesus Speaks Today

If our life's to be worthwhile
We must really learn to care,
Gladly go that extra mile,
Others joys and sorrows share.
Jesus says to us today,
I have shown you all My way.

If we really want to live
And find life abundantly,
We must first learn how to give
Out of love and sympathy.
Jesus says to us today,
For you I gave life away.

If we really want to care,
Let His life our pattern be;
By our words and actions show
Kindness and humility.
Jesus says to us today,
Lowly service is the way.

Lord, we want to live for Thee.
Grant us purpose, power and love,
Give us grace to persevere
Till we reach our home above.
Jesus says to us today,
Through the grave I led the way.

So, for us to live is Christ
And to die, for us is gain;
If we here have Him confessed,
We shall life in Heaven attain.
Lord, we say to You today,
Saviour, please show us the way.
Kathleen B Hutchings

At Peace

Along a country path, I walk at peace;
My soul in tune with everything,
The birds, the trees, the sky, the breeze
All speak and sing,
And welcome me as one of them.
Yes! One of them I feel to be,
Because God made them all and
likewise me;
And so when on a country path I plod,
I am at peace; I am with God.

Geoffrey Gostick

Life

In the folds of night's cloak
Mary shivers,
Stark in the dark
faces move as lanterns flicker
candles guttering.
She sees dimly the forms of
cattle
their breath fumes fog in a
beam of moonlight
Pain follows pain
then again
At last a birth-cry from the
straw
Her voice hushes the wailing
Creator is created.

Marion Houghton

To a White Violet
(For Mother on Mothering Sunday, 1985, based on Psalm 15)

Who shall ascend the holy hill
But you, the purest flower of spring?
Clad like an angel all in white
Without a stain of sin.

No one planted you
But He who rose in white
From out the grave
As you the earth.

Your scent is delicate and rare
Like Mary's nard for Jesus' feet:
A perfume to embalm
The corpse of winter.

You greet the rising sun with joy -
An acolyte of simple mien
Who kneels in lowly site
Espied by pilgrims to the heavenly flame.

Raised are the humble, and so are you,
Perfect creation of our Lord,
Cherished through ages past and still to come,
Found but by those who choose the hidden path.

Joy Hedges

The Reason Why

Our Creator made the Universe according to His Plan.
He made the stars; the planets; earth - and then created man.
And man looked round and saw the birds; the animals and trees.
The mountains, and the rivers flowing swiftly to the seas.
The flowers in their proud display; bright petals, velvet soft.
The sweep of sky, the towering cliffs, where sea birds wheeled aloft
He heard the music of the sea as the silver moon dipped low;
The sun blaze up at dawn to bathe God's world in golden glow.

And man walked on, bewildered. Wondering why.

He walked alone among the trees that whispered with each passing breeze.
He heard a voice; it called his name. Soft, beyond the trees it came;
And came again. He waited there. Then gently in the whispering air
It spoke...

'I created all the Universe according to My Plan.
I made the stars; the planets, earth. And then created man.
That man may carry on the work I started from above.
Of spreading Peace and Happiness; of passing on My Love.
That man might have compassion for the ones who need his care.
To help the more unfortunate their suffering to bear.
I gave him brain, and caring hands; that he might work and pray.
And I will help and guide him through every passing day.'

And man walked on, contented. Knowing why.

Genevieve Grewer

The Practice of Prayer

Sometimes I think that I have never prayed,
Apart from those occasions when my prayer
Met, made connection, found an answering voice.
For me, alas, such happenings are rare.

And yet they come. No warning, no advice,
No trick to make them come, unless it be
The lack of expectation, and the need
Which in itself implies expectancy.

And so, I pray. Too often mere routine,
Yet I accept the practice and the plod,
Till I stretch out my hand in empty need
And find it clasped within the hand of God.

Paul Scott

Peace

How do you search for something, yet unseen?
How do you reach a place you've never been?
How do you still the turmoil in your heart
Or mend a world about to fall apart?

Is there a path to follow through the pain?
Can any truth make sense of life again?
Will darkness ever be unlocked by light
Or day replace the dread of endless night?

What futile waste we see through war and greed
When envy and revenge become man's creed.
But God can take the anger from man's life
And join the hands of those once torn in strife.

The noise and clamour of our daily grind
Can quickly banish Jesus from our mind.
But He desires to dwell within us all
And be our sweet oasis when we call.

Sometimes our anguish lies too deep for tears.
We have no way to quell the crushing fears,
Except we give them over to the Lord
Who'll work with us to see our lives restored.

The price was paid at Calvary long ago
To bring the peace He wants us all to know.
If only we will let Him reign within
As we acknowledge and discard our sin.

Have you ever heard His knock upon your door,
Or wished you'd let Him enter in before?
He's waiting now to make your heart His throne.
Be still and know - He wants you for His own.
Sue Richards

Jericho Road

He heard the shouting and the distant voices' blur,
Lifted his sightless eyes to feel their load.
The crowd was coming nearer, and the sound
Burdened the beggar on the dry and dusty road.
He turned to catch the people's passing cry,
But felt the wind's sharp mocking steal each word.
What name was it the throng was echoing now?
Who walked his way? He neither saw nor heard.
'Who passes by?' he shouted as the mob came close,
He felt the flurry of their garments as they jostled near.
They pushed him to the ground, with jarring pain,
He felt his blood - and they regardless of his fear.
One tossed an answer - 'Jesus of Nazareth comes!' and could this be?
The blind man shaken by his fall staggered to stand,
Then with some inner strength he screamed in urgency
And pain of all he could not see, his eyes, his soul,
'Oh Son of David, mercy! Mercy now on me!'
The crowd pressed on, 'How dare he raise his voice,'
'Silence!' they spat, and 'Hold your tongue!' they cursed,
The sightless beggar stumbled in his blackened world,
Desperately calling out again and louder even than at first.
'Bring him to me.' a voice commanded, strong and clear.
The blind man trembled as he felt the crowd's cold stare,
Then someone took his arm, led him through all the crush
To take him to the one called Jesus standing there
Who asked him his request, - the beggar gasped, 'Help me to see!'
Then into blindness Jesus' words blazed light,
Vibrance of colour, clarity of form and line, pattern and shape,
'Receive your sight!'

Ruth Nickerson

Souls Immortal

Souls immortal, spirits unchained,
Unseen, untouchable,
What sphere doth hold beneath her sway
This great majority.

What finds the seeker of your world
In book, in voice, or dream?
Knowledge is void and vision dim
Of your existence now.

What thoughts sublime, what kindly deeds
Now shaped within your power?
Our spirits years to fathom all
To lift the veil between.

What heights to soar, fettered no more
By earthly hinderences,
What depth of love and deepening joy
Unknown, undreamt of here.

Thyself to live in God's own theme
One sound in harmony,
Where discord hath no voice to raise
In God's own melody.

Earth-born are we and earthly too
Our thoughts and schemes combined
What part have we to air or join
In that Immortal band?

Joyce Walker

Is There Sweet Music?

Is there sweet music from the daffodil
Too high to register on human ears?
Can there be octaves from the thrush's bill
That if we heard their notes, would draw our tears?

Do the stars sing throughout the cosmic sphere,
Making their harmony for Heaven alone?
A song of grasses growing, fresh and clear,
May this be heard quite plainly from the Throne?

Can God hear music from the ocean bed
Beyond the mind of man to preconceive?
And does the morning chant when night has sped,
While Sun and Moon their salutations breathe?

Who orchestrates these high exquisite sounds?
Do angels edit them the livelong day?
The noise of nations must be out-of-bounds
In this ethereal realm beyond our clay.

And yet, perhaps, when we are fast asleep
All innocent of every other thought,
Across the surface of our mental deep
May come a melody that God has wrought.

E Gwendoline Keevill

Crossroads

Torn between two worlds,
The way of living and of death
Stranded in the middle,
Undecided between right and left.

Which way to go?
To God or man?
To Heaven or to Hell?
To walk in the light
Or live in the dark?
Who knows? Who cares? Who can tell?

Standing at the crossroads
Looking for eternal life -
Take the wide and easy pathway,
The one without fear or strife.

Or there's the small and narrow road
With bumps, ditches, holes and bends,
Where life is full of troubles
But God's with you to the end.

Rachel Evans

Untitled

10/10 for antipollution
But why do we war against our creation

A quiet glint came to my eye
Was I the plank on the watery mud
Did I obstruct the way of love
Oh no, not I but eye.

At the last sigh of the spinning jenny,
The maid set down her JMA penny
It was all the wages of the day
Oh to be poor, for rich was He

Signed, sealed, rolled up and wrapt,
Here the answer, the most, the very apt
The gap twixt man and God between sealed
The scroll, the covenant of Jesus' deal

Just as small as the favourite tree,
Just as high as the line post be.
He the King who wrought creation
Died on wood for every nation.

Love is true about the Lord
Conquering Christ and loving Lord
He's a master over sin
His victories are felt within - within our heart.

R Shawcroft

Nicodemus to the Wind

I cry your mercy, wind, tonight:
Dare not gainsay, defy, your might.
Your gusty maniac merriment,
Guffawing down the chimney-vent,
Would make phlegmatic mountains shake
And hidden layers of ocean quake.

Times you have piped a whistle through the window-slits,
My heart has danced to laughter-fits.
But when, with ruthless giant force
You blow my thinking off its course,
Fill every fastness with a vast unease,
Rending my rooted stillness as you wrench the trees,
I cry your non-existent mercy, cower,
Fearing your huge dispassionate power.

For whence you come and whither you go
Is more than mortal man may know.

Muriel Taylor

Kneel Before the Cross

If you're feeling low in spirit and your day is without hope,
If you're worship fails to uplift you and enable you to cope,
Stop thinking of the problems of the things you've gained or lost,
Get back to the beginning and kneel before the cross.
And bring to mind the picture of the Saviour hanging there,
Bruised and battered, bleeding, hurt and sad and bare,
A crown of thorns upon his head, mingling blood and sweat and tears,
The crowds who came to see this Jew their shouts and boos and jeers,
And look upon that body, robbed of dignity and pride,
Its broken limbs, its wounded flesh, the pierce down one side,
The hands which did surrender to each cruel wooden nail,
The body left to die in pain hanging limp and frail.
And in that damaged body stripped of everything but pain,
See new hope for the future and the will to try again,
Feel humble as you see the cost, the price that Jesus paid,
To free us from the pain of sin that sacrifice he made.
So if your Christian life causes frustration and despair,
You're running round in circles to find answers that aren't there,
If you're losing track of what's the truth and feeling at a loss,
Get back to the beginning and kneel before the cross.

Nicola Benn

Untitled

In quiet contemplation
I find you
In hasty daytime-life
I forget you
In the still evening-time
I remember you...

... And feel ashamed
That I was too busy
To notice
That my closest Friend
Was patiently waiting
For me

You quietly forgive
The abuse of the relationship
I committed
Knowing always that
Tomorrow may be the same
For us...

... In the morning sunrise
I'll see You
In the whispering breeze
I'll hear You
In the warmth of the noontide
I'll feel You...

... Whilst in the night-time
In humble penitence
I'll simply love You.

Chris Coupe

Miracles Happen

Miracles happen on every day,
A falling star, or lambs at play,
A flower gleams through melting snow
And a Robin sings, bright breast aglow.
A duckling swims within hours of birth,
Circling in space revolves the earth.

Miracles happen on any day,
Spring turns to Summer in the month of May,
And every flowering tree doth shed
Sweet blossoms to make a downy bed,
To cushion the fruit that later will fall,
Somehow the children have grown so tall!

Miracles happen on any day,
For all your gifts:- Oh Lord I pray,
From a praising and a thankful heart,
Teach me Dear God to play my part,
That I might assist in the scheme of things
And serving, know the Joy it brings.

Miracles happen on every day,
Already, Oh Lord, you've shown the way,
To live our lives for this brief span,
When you came to earth as God made Man,
We believe you atoned for all our sin
To Heaven, Your presence, may we enter in.

Miracles happen on Easter day,
And all God's children who've gone astray
Are offered forgiveness at His side.
To share His Calvary where He died,
Then rise to Heaven, with Him for ever,
From whose presence no man can sever.
A H Shepherd

Giving Till it Hurts

Almost ashamed she felt
Standing in the donations queue.
A small amount was more than
She could afford for refugees,
Towns destroyed and flooded;
Starvation, disease; fleeing from war.

That man in front, all Havana smoke,
And a Jag, round the corner;
Then off for a tipple:
The big amount he gave
Would not ripple his credit.
Did he disdain her little
Handful of silver?...

But then, our Lord, she thought,
Wasn't rich, either. No money
In the Bank for Him.
Yet he gave all He had: His life.

Frank Morley

Mere Mortal

there are miles of stone here in our cathedrals
we have built them of miles,
like the light years we take to reach God
a thousand thousand thousand is like nothing
and you - little grain of dust -
you breathe and you live
and you think you know what living is
but you are like a speck in the eye
not even the mote;

but not even the miles, the light years
or the eye can possibly contain
what God is
was
shall be
what love is
you might just have the very slightest inkling
mere mortal.

Liz Knowles

Jesus Meets Us

Our glorious resurrection
From the tomb Our Lord is free
God raises His beloved Son
The Christ of Calvary.

Jesus Our Lord is risen
Is alive for evermore
Through death and resurrection
The ever open door.

The one despised, rejected
And wounded for all our sin
Bruised for our iniquities
All hearts of men to win.

Christians now for this rejoice
No more shall the Saviour die
Salvation is perfected
Now recall the Baptists cry.

Behold the Lamb of God
Who shall bear our iniquity
This He has done, praise His name
And won the victory.

As he meets you this Easter
Like on the Emmaus road
With Mary in the garden
The truth He will unfold.

Eric Wyld

A Hymn

To set aright a world we now despise,
To seek a peace which none can understand
To know no fear of battles in the skies,
This is the peace we cherish, seek, demand.

Goodwill toward all men we do desire,
This is the hope for which all humans toil;
We ask for patience, health, strength to inspire
Men's thoughts to keep mad warfare from our soil.

God made man's dwelling-place so wondrous fair
So many beauteous things to please the eye;
Oh, pause and ponder on the Father's care
Of all things living under His blue sky.

Season will follow season, come what may
God's laws are kept both this and every day,
May nations seek belief in God, and pray
His love may guide them in the noblest way.

Lord, give us patience to endure the strife;
To search for beauty, harmony and peace;
Thy gift of love illuminate our life
Proving thy care for us doth never cease.

Audrey J Sizer

Belonging

In warmth of hearth, for some, Belonging lies;
Some wed themselves to work; but some embrace
Delight in sensual snares,
Grim tomb where longing dies.

So tenuous our link with heaven's song,
So frail our contact with eternity;
We hear the songs of earth
Enticing to belong.

But when the chips are down, and desolate
We drift alone with fear and shattered dreams,
When silence screams it's curse,
Whence comes our advocate?

Not from our triumphs in the ways we've trod,
Nor recollections of our richest joys,
Our need belongs beyond
And reaches back to God.

Our hurts drive deep, beyond the well of tears,
Into the heart of God where we belong
With Christ, who took our hurts
'midst cries, and Cross, and spears.

All our belongings are but sips, of wine
That flows from God, and filled the heart of Christ;
Our hung'rings to belong reach for the bread
That clothed our Lord that night of Eucharist.

'Abide with me' He said, 'And I in you';
This, this is the beginning and the end
Of all our deepest longings to belong
When, held in love no fear can apprehend,
Our life transcends this life, and joyous gives
Itself away, clasped by the Christ who lives.

R Kemp

Worthy the Lamb

How solemn is this awful fact concerning everyone.
God's wrath abides upon us unless we trust His Son;
But if we come in repentance and believe for us He died
God looks on us as found in Him and we are justified.
Then as He has begun a good work in our lives He will
go on and perfect it from henceforth until
He presents us faultless in God the Father's sight,
Changed into His likeness, clad in garments white.
Then what a song we'll sing to Him to whom we owe it all,
'Worthy the Lamb' we'll cry as we prostrate before Him fall.

Kathleen Pike

Letting Go

If, when I see you pray
My eyes caress the hair upon your nape
And probe the gentle shadows of your hand
Hiding your eyes,
Then I must worship blind,
Pluck out the twining visions of my mind
And damn the course of my imaginings.
So must I grope before my God, eyeless.

Your voice still lifts in prayer,
Desire turns back to linger as you plead,
Blending voices raised to heaven assault.
But I am mute.
I cannot say Amen,
Rather seal this mouth from cursing or with
These hands tear out the clapper from the bell.
So must I crouch before my God, voiceless.

And while you kneel in prayer
I warm my stiffened limbs, now wanting you
To know my meaning, know my feeling.
A woe too great.
A word not to be fleshed.
Sightless, voiceless, wordless before my God.
Is only hearing left, last sense to go?
Through grace, because you love, now let him go.

Alisoun M Ward

Shopping for a God

Please remember always
when shopping for a God
That some things in your trolley
may turn out to be quite odd
Aromatherapy and crystals
may be all the rage
with bits of older religions
in a package called New Age
But will they really bring you
the fulfilment that you seek?
or are they being hyped up
as bargains of the week?
It's an easy spirituality
that's being put on sale
you are God and powerful
so what happens when *you* fail?
There are no sins to repent of
no-one higher to obey
No moral codes to adhere to
but is that the best way?
Jesus is Almighty God,
yet is also friend
He loves, comforts, transforms us
and is with us to the end
Could you say the same thing
about the *God* of your choice?
Even if it's the TV set
or your brand new Rolls Royce!
Probably the decision
is not as easy as you thought
but I hope you'll be satisfied
with the religion that you've bought!

Linda Smith

See Here I Am...

When faint and weak, the spirit quails
And stumbles to her knees;
When all around is dark and cold -
And only grief she sees;
When all seems friendless bleak and drear,
And faith has fallen low;
Then gently comes, on wings of peace,
The Spirit of His love and grace,
And hears the words: 'Oh precious child
See, here I am - I do love you'.

Once empty, now, is filled again -
Her failing strength renewed;
And yearning with her love for Him
She reaches upward now;
And all her trust she gives to Him -
And all her suffering too -
And wonderingly she sees again,
His sunshine gleaming through the rain,
And hears His words: 'Oh precious child
See, here I am - I do love you'.

H Collins

Pilgrimage

Lord, once you called me in my days of youth,
And I responded in my callow way;
I knew not how to worship you in truth,
And eagerly mis-served you day by day.
Yet you accepted service so uncouth,
As, stumblingly, I entered life's affray.

The years have passed and each its portion brought,
Of modest gain or of forgiven loss;
The youth to manhood grew, yet ever sought
To know full meaning of your saving cross,
Until your Spirit, in God's wisdom taught,
Without your love all earthly things are gross.

Help me to yield the life that you have made,
Whether its essence be of gain or loss;
A life that's useful, satisfying and unpaid,
At least by earth's poor gold and silver dross.
For memory of earthly recompense will fade,
But not the knowledge that I shared your cross.

Make me a heart responsive to your love;
Give me a mind that bases all on you;
May my poor will be strengthened from above,
That I may do the things you'd have me do.
Then, when I cease this earthly paradise to rove,
Take me to share eternal life with you.

O Burchill

A Christmas Rap

Yo listen up people, I've got something to say,
'Bout the time and place of Jesus' Birthday.
It started one night in Bethlehem,
Mary and Joseph in a stable then.
The angel came into sight,
It gave the shepherds a great big fright.
Then three Kings came all chubby and fat,
They came up to Joseph and had a chat.
Brought along Myrrh, Frankincense and Gold,
And that's just about the story told.
But don't go away 'cos I got something to say
And I wanna say it here
Have a very merry Christmas and a happy New Year!

Ellen Ralls (8)

My Emmaus

When I walk with Him He talks with me
Explaining how life ought to be
I see Him, yet I simply don't see
Why He should bother with the likes of me.

Confused, confounded, concussed by life,
He picks me up, dusts me down, turns me around,
Points in a new direction, offering wisdom to follow the way.
Ashamed, astounded, atoned by grace.

Yet for so long I didn't recognise, so long I would flee,
So long I didn't know, so long I wasn't free.
So long I was running directionless, I couldn't see
Chasing shadows and illusions, valueless to me.

Overcome, overawed, overwhelmed with thanks
With new life, new hope and new purpose.
The shutters lifted from my eyes, showing everything in true perspective,
Rejoicing, rejuvenating, released by love.

Patrick Sherring

Gethsemane

I dreamed my lover came to me
With scented kisses in a garden full of flowers,
Secretly.
By night he came and stole away my breath,
And swore his faithful vows of love to keep
Till death.
But then I dreamed my lover went away
And left me crying in the empty, tear-stained dawn
Of day.
I looked for him along the paths of sleep,
Full overgrown with heavy-hearted loss,
My wounds cut deep.
Yet as I called his name, and wept,
My hope grew cold, although my love still burned.
But as I slept,
I found myself awakening from the night -
I dreamed I saw the garden once again; my heart
Grew light.
A figure kneeling there, so hushed of tone
I barely heard the sorrow in his deep
And anguished groan.
Not here the elusive lover that I vainly sought,
But something purer, blazing as a cleansing fire -
Of Heaven wrought.
And here I found Him in His agony,
Willing to give His all that I might live. I found my lover
In Gethsemane.

Sarah J Honour

The Open Door

Build a house, stone upon stone.
A house to share, not yours alone.
Make it's foundation strong and secure.
A place for the rich as well as the poor.
A place not just to congregate
For a neighbourly chat, a tete-a-tete,
But open the door to the passer by,
The doubting Thomas, the blind of eye.
Those who have never known the truth,
Who can't believe, for lack of proof.
So why not you to show the way,
Invite them in, urge them to stay.
Faith knows no bounds, you have the key,
Use it with efficiency.
God will be there, He'll be your guide,
Once those in doubt have stepped inside.

Nancy Morley

The True Vine

When Jesus was teaching His followers,
he said, 'I am the True Vine,
The Gardener, is God the Father
And you, the branches are Mine.'

The Vine that God planted upon the Earth,
Is the Root from which Life flows,
And from many of its branches
A shoot flourished and grows.

But a tree that bears fruit will need pruning,
And dead branches cut away.
If we abide in Jesus,
His commandments we must obey.

The severed branches will wither and die,
And the others God will trim,
To make them clean and more fruitful,
That they may grow strong in Him.

We are cleansed by the shed blood of Jesus,
And by the power of His word.
Jesus said, 'Love one another,
That your joy be complete in God.'

When we share in the Holy Communion
And receive the bread and wine,
Remember the beautiful picture
That Christ *painted* of the vine.

Mavis Tebby

Candle - Light at Willen

The flame burns pure:
a single symmetry
of curve and apex,
reaching up, in still geometry
of sustained form.

The circle contemplates
the silent flame
which stills their minds
and gives their souls a space
to house the light.

Blessed are the pure
whose inner vision
holds them true
as, wholly given,
they too burn bright.

My astigmatic eye
sees double, fraction
reflecting too well
forked mind, forked tongue
of imperfection.
But, candle in the dark,
your little flame
says: 'I shall be your light.
Be free from your self-blame.
Rest in God's sight.'

Barbara Clifton

Earth Talk, Rio, 1992
(where nations were feasted as they discussed the Third World...)

The night they all betrayed Him
He took and broke the bread.
'The more you have and hold to
The less you are,' He said.

He folded in His hands
The baking and the growing
And told them how their harvest
Came from some other's sowing.

They served their wine with sermons
As He knelt and washed their feet.
The starving stood and watched them
As they ate and ate and ate.

The poor creep in and scavenge
For the crumbs that fall too late.

Hilary Elfick

Peace

Vain is the strife, the coward and the brave
Together find their solace in the grave.
O blessed Abel, pitiable Cain no rest is thine,
Foul dreams shall haunt thy steps from early morning light
Until the advent of eternal night.

Prepare destruction for the fight for peace?
The fruit is in the seed, remember this,
Foul evil never yet did bring forth good
And canker will destroy the choicest wood.
The stoutest ships the stormy seas impound
Upon the rocks ne'er made the harbour sound.

Have you not heard, the sword shall pierce the heart of him who wealds it;
And vain is he whose trust is in the bomb;
For both together in the tomb shall lie;
Theirs is the peace of death, the peace of life
Lies in the courage which resists the strife.

F Aspin

A Poem for Good Friday

Across the darkness of the galaxies,
Lonely on a splintered cross,
The agonies of ages
Are played out on the tattered tissues
Of a frail and fragile flesh.
A lonely death, foreseen
Before the time-span of existence,
Takes shape upon a moving fragment
Of experience, and persists indelible
Through the multi layers of eternity:
Hands pinned out in agony,
Weak and defeated in a moment,
Forever shape the moral structure
Of the cosmos, as power is expressed
In pain, and forgiveness in
A stream of blood. God in Jesus
Gives meaning to the void and demonstrates
The transcendent reality of love.

Derek Lawrence

Homeless

'Walking, walking, to and fro,
Walking on.. nowhere to go
Everyone else seems bound for some place
I watch them walk.. from my slower pace.

They're off to work, or going home
Or meeting friends, while I just roam
They look forward to warmth and care
I have no-one with whom to share.

Everyone seems to have an aim
As I look on.. should I feel shame?
I've tried for work, within my scope
No fixed abode means.. *there's no hope.*

On Sundays, I watch them, leaving Church
From my favourite cardboard perch
They're kind to me with their *day-care*
But.. worship? Nothing clean to wear!

I wonder what their Lord would say
If He should now pass by my way
Somehow, I think He'd stay with *me*
For *He* was once a refugee.

Sister Jean Oglethorpe

For a Pilgrim

Lord, at the start it seemed impossible.
If only I had a map, I'd know the way to go;
I could anticipate the difficulties;
see how far I'd come
and how far left to go.

But exciting too!
There have been good days,
days full of trust and confidence and joy.
Sometimes days so good it doesn't seem to matter
that I'm still on a journey,
that I haven't yet arrived.

But I need to be reminded;
I am still on the journey;
only you know the way.
You lead, I must follow.
I musn't take a different route
(perhaps a shortcut)
... and arrive at a different destination.

Sometimes I wonder what I'm doing
so far from home.
Wouldn't it be safer to turn around?
To go back?
But that would be to stop trusting.

Did you feel like that in Gethsemane?
In spite of all that had gone before?
Did the Father really want you to die?
To lay down your life, with so much left to do?
Or was this just your own special kind of ego trip?
And rising again - that must have seemed a crazy idea!
And no-one to give you a map
or tell you how they'd done it before.

So much simpler,
so much safer
to go back home - to Nazareth.
'Very sensible,' they'd all say,
(and wouldn't your mother be pleased).

Lord, *Not my will, but yours.*
Help me do the impossible.

George Brigham

Comparison

I cannot understand the love of Jesus,
Or plumb the depths of mercy, full and free.
To know that every hair of mine is numbered,
And every sin is cast beneath the sea.

I cannot reach the standards met by others,
My feet are prone to stumble on the way.
So many good intentions seem to crumble,
I seldom choose the wisest things to say.

The wonder is He loves and still accepts me,
In spite of all the faults that He can see.
He never once withdraws the love He gave me,
Just what has this to say to me?

Because He loves, then I must show to others,
the same concern and loving care received.
Consideration, faith and trust, compassion,
Minister to each and every need.

They will not understand the love of Jesus,
Except that love flow out for all to see.
Convincing them by word and deed and action,
He cares for them, just like He cares for me.

Rosemary Payne

Seeing is Believing

The heathered hills
Seemed stroked with sorrow
As the day's clouds crept overhead
And brought great brows of darkness;
Hills of black and blue and purple,
Lumped together worryingly,
Harrying and harrowing the land
As if battered by the hand of God.

Thinking on God seemed natural there
Even though it was ordinary enough.
In fact the ordinariness made it
More special
Somehow.

I found myself asking
What seemed like others' questions,
yet it seemed like I should be answering.
It seemed like the plain hills were interrogating me.

Everything seemed special -
Even the matter-of-factness:
The special in the ordinary
The wild in the tamed.

Walter Riggans

Easy Religion

I want an easy religion,
One that gives me freedom.
No bondage, free to be me;
Whatever I am,
Whoever I am.
Whenever I am.

I want an easy religion,
One that give me no laws.
No binding boundaries;
Whatever I am,
Whoever I am,
Whenever I am.

I want an easy religion,
One that gives me no demands.
Just many choices;
Whatever I am,
Whoever I am,
Whenever I am.

I want an easy religion,
So I will listen to Jesus.
He has an easy religion to follow:
At least, many of His followers
Seem to act as though it is so;
Whatever they are,
Whoever they are,
Whenever they are.

A B Mossta

Untitled

Hugged within creepered walls a sorrowing splendour
Whispers its gentle epitaph of grief;
This, Joseph's sanctuary where he lingers
To seek oblivion in unbelief.

Here by the tomb, heads bowed, the lilies standing,
Keep watch as by a royal catafalque,
The poppies, spilled like droops of blood, are glowing
'Gainst barren rock beside each sheltered walk.

A woman's last low sob, retreating footsteps,
In silence all earth's tiny creatures mourn;
Blinded by tears, despairing, Joseph stumbles,
Stoops and picks up a coronet of thorn.

But wait - a new exultant joy is dawning,
Sad desolate Gethsemane will sing;
Flowers, trees and people shout aloud rejoicing
For He is here - no gardener but our King.

Mary Graves

Good Friday Thoughts on Christmas

Where are all those who worshipped at the cradle
When bid we them to worship at the Cross.
So few are they who crowded to the stable
Who say, 'For this I count the world but loss.'

Where are all those who gazed into the manger
When Calvary's Cross is all our focus now?
Is He who hangs in sacrificial pain a stranger?
Will they who knelt at birth, not at His death all bow?

Aubrey Ridge

Praying Time

When it is dark and I cannot sleep,
When I have too much to do,
When I am lost, unsure where to go,
That's when I pray to you.

When I'm in trouble, sad or in pain,
When life seems uncertain, untrue,
When people are angry and work is hard,
That's when I pray to you.

But when life is easy and things go well,
There seems less time for you.
So please God forgive me and help me to see,
At these times I should pray too.

I know you are with me always,
You're in all my thoughts, all I do,
But still I should daily spend time in prayer
To say 'Father, I really thank you'.

Rachel J Sparks

As a Child

I came, as a child, when love grieved me,
To a place which was quiet and alone;
Behind a closed door I could think and restore
And weigh up - my sins to atone.

I went there all drained and guilt-laden
With tears welling up in my eyes;
I talked to the Lord and he heard me
While dealing with Satan's cruel lies.

My heart came, so heavy and hopeless;
I knelt at His feet to receive.
He said 'I am here, child, just listen;
I love you and know how you grieve.'

'You have sinned, yes, in some ways I blame you;
I'm a God who won't tolerate sin.
But now you have chosen the good thing -
You have opened the door - I've come in.'

I came as a child when love grieved me
To a place which was quiet and lone;
I was then scarce aware of a Saviour
Who was eager for sins to atone.

Now my heart's more mature but still open
To all life can do to destroy;
But in that quiet place, heart heavy as lead,
Lies always a tear-spattered joy;
For God came to weep for our failures,
He's there to bear all grief and pain;
And surrendered to Him, cleansed, released now,
I walk in the sunshine again.

Sheila Winson

The Christ of the Burned Men
(for Thomas Merton)

See them.
Limping from the secret place of their God,
Consumed and entranced,
Addicts of the divine.

Their strength is wasting away.
Proud, human energy
Burned out in this
Crucible of love and torture.
See them.

They have tasted a hidden fire,
Seen a secret sight.
They are burning and burning
In a terrible heat.
The agony and the beauty of the Lord
Has touched them.
Observe.

Like those arthritic before old age
They move slowly, stumbling,
His pain in their blood and joints.
Their faces are blazing,
Shining with a passion too vibrant for the casual,
Too subtle for the observer of the obvious.
Attend.

Their pyre lights the dark places,
And melts the glacier heart of man.

Tim Marks

Church on Sundays

If I could face the aftermath
I would take my cup
(coffee, one sugar)
and hurl it
right across the hall.
I could watch it break,
sweet liquid
spatter down the wall,
and crash and smash
in pieces too small
to make again.
The ensuing mess
would rob me of my rage
and sweeping it away
we would pretend
we could pretend.

Ann Page

Senses

Lord, I nearly lost my eyes
In the dark days without warning.
Thank You for allowing me to see again
hidden beauties of Your world.

Lord, I nearly lost my ears
In wild clamourings of the selfish.
Thank You for letting me hear clearly
the cries of Your lonely, lost flock.

Lord, I nearly lost my taste
for the depth and meaning of being.
Thank You for the tang of salt and foam
but mostly for my zestful taste for life.

Lord, I nearly lost my smell
in the mire of treachery and oppression.
Thank You for the smell
of brotherly warmth on a Winter's day.

Lord, I nearly lost my touch
for two-ness and communication.
thank You also for the quiet times
when You touched me with Your presence.

Lord, I nearly lost my way
in the mazes of want and greed.
Thank You for reminding me
that You are there and I am here.

Lord,

Thank You for bringing me to my senses.

Gerry Brown

Corpus Christi

Today I went open-handed
and empty-hearted,
to God.
Bare of feeling,
stripped of desire.

What was placed
into my open, empty
hands?
Bread and wine?
Doctrine and Tradition?
Blind faith?
Or a transfusion of living hope?

Of themselves
my hands shaped over wafer and wine
the sign of crucifixion.
Ultimate emptiness,
Complete openness,
Powerlessness
with power
to grant meaning
to the meaningless.

I did not feel new life
thrilling through me.
But the prayed-in peace
of ancient stone
held me,
And the faith-soaked words
caressed me,
And the look and the touch of the man of God
moved me,
And I am glad that I went
emtpy-handed to God
and ate and drank
of Corpus Christi

Veronica Faulks

Riches

Self whispered, 'You are rich,
All these you have begotten:
Comforting walls of home,
Soft-shaded lighting, carpets
Fitted and gentle to the tread;
Indoor plants, a garden
Safe in trimmed hedges,
Private and aloof.
Music, books, the joys of art.
Sessions in fellowship
That glow with earnest thought.
The lines have fallen in pleasant places
And you are rich indeed.'

Self whispered, 'Are you rich?
So much you have forgotten.
These things are but a mask
Veiling the striving of a soul
Stifled and unfulfilled
Unless she breaks the bond
Of well-being
And ventures forth
To find her greater counterpart
Upon a cross that lies
Athwart a suffering world.'
I cried, 'Lord, break this bond and set me free
For I am poor indeed.'

Dorothy Woo

Them

As I listen to the crowd on a train, a bus, in the shops,
or a multitude of other places
The theme is always *them*

It's *them* who cause the strikes, bad workmanship and
the rising rate of crime
The appliances that break down and the failures on the line

It's *them* who are so lazy and never did want work
And *them* who get rich quick and are living off their perks

It's *them* who are so wrong and never in the right
Who fail to make the grade, who I regularly indite

It's *them* who are the majority - why I'll never see
'Oh Lord I'm nearly perfect, please make them more like me.'

And God said 'All have sinned and are far from my saving presence.'
'But Lord, surely some have sinned more seriously then others.'
And God said 'All have sinned and are far from my saving presence.'
I began to see that all people were the same in His sight and
read further '... but by the *Free gift of God's grace* we
are all put right through Jesus Christ who sets us free'

Oh Lord, may I receive your gift and may I recognise
Your grace and not judge others. May I see that you love
all people without discrimination. Help me to remember
this in all my dealings with men and women and show something
of your love to all I meet.

Alan Sourbut

Pilgrimage

April was coming
and my soul thirsted
to drink from the Holy Grail.
I cast off the cords of brotherly love.
I flew with the invisible man
to the town of St George and oranges.

We went up to Jerusalem
into the labyrinth.
'Our home,' he said 'Follow Me.'
He led me into a desert of carved and coloured stones.
'Do you give me these for bread?'
'Lift up your eyes and look.'
We shared the horizon together.
Moriah of dove-drawing death
Zion of spiritual praise
The empty skull of knowledge
The olive mountain of ascending pain.
'These the four walls I knew,
and you must know them too.'

Thence to the Gentile circle
about the mystic lake
pouring its waters of life and truth
into the sea of death.
'This is the Twelve's classroom.'
And I gazed at the visual aids.

I climbed in the sevenfold footsteps
of the corpse whom Satan desired.
Thence to the land of St George.
'You discovered?' my brother questioned.
And I gave him the answer 'Yes.'

C J E Lefroy

Two Bowls of Water

Two bowls of water, with source in common spring.
Fresh, cool, clear, clean
Inwardly to refresh, outwardly to cleanse.

One bowl is for dirty feet
The other is for hands already clean.

Which water is polluted after washing?
Which is made impure by contact with the flesh?
Which has lost the lustre of its native power?

The feet of the disciples washed by Jesus' hands?
The hands of Pilate washed by his own hands?

One used in the acceptance of humble service?
Once used to abdicate one's charge?

One sincere, the other cynical?
one, his manner humble. The other's manner haughty -

One self-giving? One self seeking?

One aroused by inward motivation?
One propelled by forces from outside?

One taking matters into his own hands?
One evading his role to choose and to decide?

One is innocent, but charged with guilt?
One is guilty, pleading innocence?

I know which water I should choose, but do I always choose it?
What answer would you have me give?
The one expected, nay demanded by my faith?
Or the answer nearer to the heart of things that really are?

Give me Lord, the water used for feet.
The water of service and humility
May it be for ever fresh, for ever cool, for ever clear, for ever clean;
Unlike the water I disown, reject.
Not the water polluted by the hands of Pilate
But the water purified by you.

Malcolm Beech

Alive

Alive to all the agony,
      the pain, the thirst, the hungry eyes,
         the shock, the strain, the empty hands,
One question stabs,
One question burns,
Is there a God above?

Alive to all the ecstasy,
      the joy, the thrill, the glazing eyes,
         the gasps, the groans, the clenching hands,
One question stabs,
One questions burns,
Is there a God of love?

Alive to all the tragedy,
      the cross, the thorns, the upturned eyes,
         the tears, the tomb, the outstretched hands,
One question stabs,
One question burns,
Is there a God at all?

Alive to pain and agony,
Alive to joy and ecstasy,
Alive in every tragedy,
Alive when anguish plumbs the depths,
Alive when passion scales the heights,
Alive, Alive, always Alive,
He lives, he loves, he is.

And so,
Because he is Alive,
He lives, he loves, he ever is,
In Christ I trust.

Michael Saward

Empathy

I talk, they listen but the mind is blind,
to grasp, to feel all in my mind,
How to pass on the meaning for them to find?
Oh Friend please hear but not be blind.

I scurry for words but feel no magnet,
Between me and them just a cold white blanket,
Help me O Lord to break the silence,
Between me and them those friends with patience.

Simon Horn

Why Me

Sitting here in my pew, dreaming away,
Trying hard not to listen to the preacher today.
I've got enough troubles to weight me down,
Without hearing of Jesus and His thorny crown.

I've been made redundant, new jobs are rare,
So don't make me picture Him hanging up there.
I look around at the faces, the different expressions,
Some smiling, some thoughtful, while I feel depression.

The preacher still goes on, I've heard it before,
He's telling us that Jesus knocks on our door.
Well I've never heard Him, He musn't have been
Can't say as I blame Him, I'm bad company.

But who am I kidding? I heard Him knock,
I didn't want to answer, my heart was like rock.
So I stayed by myself, built a big wall,
No step of faith for me, so frightened I'd fall.

But Jesus was stubborn, He wanted to stay,
And as I built my wall He took it away .
So I let Him come in, into my life
To share all my troubles, ease my strife.

But now I feel guilty for letting Him down,
I feel that I've hurt Him, like that thorny crown.
But still He forgives me, for causing Him pain,
Till my fragile faith comes together again.

Tom Luke

Scattered Seed

There, in a crack beside the door,
a weed had grown and flowered
and, in its season, cast its seeds upon the wind
to settle in some distant spot.
Some were wasted, trodden underfoot,
and some were eaten by the hungry birds,
but some found earth and sent down roots
to gather nourishment for shoots
which grew toward the sun
and, in their turn, produced their flowers and seeds
and so achieved the great Creator's plan.

And what of those who gathered week by week within these walls
to offer prayers and praises and feed upon the Word of God?
They too have scattered far and wide
in search of food and water for their souls.
Some have fallen by the way,
turning to material things to satisfy their needs,
denying thirst for living water from eternal springs,
until they thirst no more.
But some have sought and found a place
in rich and fertile ground, a spiritual home
where, nurtured, they can grow toward the Son
who, in due season, brings forth the Spirit's fruit,
that God's will may be done.

Jesus said, 'This is to my Father's glory, that you bear much fruit,
showing yourselves to be my disciples.' (John 15v.8)

Christine Hope

Shine On Jesus

There's a darkness
Ruling over the earth,
There's a message
Of fear and despair.

There's a feeling
Of hatred, around the world,
There's a cloud
Of doubt everywhere.

But look, look, look up to heaven,
Look, see the light from above,
Come crashing down
To open our eyes,
With a message of hope and of love.
It's Jesus, shining, bright and clear,
It's the son of God winning through.
He's quelling the anger and healing the pain,
Taking away all the tears and the shame,
Bringing a rainbow to shine through our rain.
Jesus is shining for you.

Roy L Barber

Temptation

Now is the time when I have to be strong,
Now is the time when I must stand alone.
Now, at my weakest, I come to You, Lord,
Give me the strength of Your comforting word.
You know my secrets my fear and my pain;
You know my feelings, and yet You remain;
Still by my side, as a friend, strong and true:
Now in my darkness, I turn, Lord, to You.
Show me Your light for each step of the way.
May I depend on Your presence today.
Grant me Your armour, the enemy sees
All of my weaknesses; when on my knees
I come to You at the end of the day:
Help me, in truth, to be able to say:
I have not yielded to fear or to pain,
Nor to temptation; and let me remain
Close by your side, though the world thinks I stand,
Lone and defenceless; I have at my hand:
Strength from above that I know will not fail,
Your mighty power and Your truth will prevail.

Grace S Edgoose

Veronica

Legend tells how Veronica was so distressed by the sight of Christ carrying His cross to Calvary that she ran from the crowd to wipe His sweating face. On the cloth was left the image of His features. A cloth purporting to be 'Veronica's veil' is preserved in St Peter's at Rome.

High sun consumes the minutes one by one.
He stumbles with the cross, falls, falls again
on unrelenting earth; the jolt of pain
convulses all my thoughts, a storm begun
in me: what I should do I do not dare.
Uneased by truth I loiter in the crowd.
No bright hosannas cheer His palmless road
where stones and flame-tongued malice scorch the air.
I glance at Him: how His dark, prescient gaze
compels! I run to wipe His face. Rage seethes
and gaping mouths accuse; but here for me,
mapped on this cloth, is Love's extremity,
the final, ravaged path I yearned to ease.
Will time, I ask, profess this never was?

Grace Nicholls

Confusion

I am young,
        I am old,
I am frail,
        I am bold.

I am sweet,
        I am sour,
I am kind,
        I am dour.

I am a child,
        I am mature,
I can be pure
        Yet act so wild.

I am a friend,
        I am a foe,
I long to love,
        But can't let go.

I seek to serve
        And am sincere
Yet all is vain
        For self holds reign.

I am a fool
        But can be wise
I am so brave
        Yet fear belies.

I am so happy
        Yet feel so sad
My heart is heavy
        But my words are glad.

But I will not despair
       Tho doubt lurks between,
For Jesus stands guard,
       His strength ... far supreme.

Margaret Godden

Blind before Him

His cry shook me.

I awoke to showering life
Which scattered my sharpened knife of hatred
And the empty blame I gave Him.
My scorn has fallen.

His back cradled me.

While I dive into the deepest Pit,
Love is the Most High,
It wins.

But Satan took hold,
He rode on me, trod on me,
I was soaked in nothing.
Yet here I am again,

Jesus loves me.

And I believe.

Emma Bateman

True Joy

When sadness fills the heart
And the world seems all awry,
If only we would lift our eyes
To see God's rainbow in the sky.
He is there when all else fails,
His promises are true,
He will lift the veil of tears,
The sun will then shine through.

When with joy the heart is filled
And the days fly all too fast,
Forget not then to lift the eyes
To gaze upon the Cross.
God sacrificed His one true Son
To save us from our sins.
That joy one day will be complete
When we sit at our Saviour's feet.

E Maisie Clegg

Christmas Bells

Christmas bells, chiming bells,
What is the story that you tell?
Is it of a crowded Inn
Where no room was found within?
Is it of a blessed mother
Lost in praise and love and wonder?
Is it of a stable bare
With the Christ child lying there?
Is it of the shepherds poor
Come to worship and adore?
Is it of a shining star
Guiding wise men from afar?
Is it of the angel song
Telling the world that Christ has come?
All these things and many more -
How Christ opened wide the door,
For all mankind to live in glory
That's the truth of the Christmas story.
Now when you hear those chiming bells
Listen to the tale they tell.

Mary Anderson

The Answer

There comes a time for most of us,
When, in darkness and despair,
We grope around for happiness,
Which simply is not there.

We long for joys we knew of old,
Times we thought would never end.
Where have they gone? We ask ourselves,
As our spirits fast descend.

Then sometime, on our darkest day,
A tiny light appears,
We begin to see things differently,
And can wipe away our tears.

We've prayed, and God has listened
Though we thought he wasn't there,
Just when we've reached our lowest ebb,
Comes an answer to our prayer.

Could be it's not the one that we
        expect to receive,
But we must trust that it is right,
And in its truth believe.

All at once our steps are lighter,
Time no longer heavy lies,
There is meaning to our life again,
God is near, we realise.

Mary Peagram

The Secret

Just like a baby asleep in his cot,
Lay a little brown bulb in a little red pot.
I carefully watched it day by day
As snug and dormant in its bed it lay.
I wondered just how long it would take
For that little brown bulb to stir and wake
To the light and the warmth of the living world,
Its leaves and petals all unfurled.
Just how would that little brown bulb come alive,
From where the germ of life derive?
I could watch and cherish and water it too,
But I couldn't make it grow what'er I might do.
The force of energy we all share,
Comes from what - comes from where?
Mankind has discovered amazing things,
But not the source from which life springs,
We can telephone and televise,
Fly Jets and Concordes across the skies.
Create a tape that records a tune,
Split the atom and walk on the moon.
Harness energy from the suns rays,
Tamper with nature in all sorts of ways.
Vast is our knowledge and great is our skill,
But that little brown bulb on my window sill
Contains a secret that none of us know.
Where does life come from - where does it go?
The answer's not ours to understand,
It's securely held in the palm of God's hand.

Marjorie Short

The Person on the Poster

I doubt if you will know me,
There are many just like me.
My face is one in millions,
One of two-in-every-three,
Who are just about surviving in a land, hard, parched and dry,
And without the food you send me, I know that I would die.

In a forest clearing,
Where the green grass used to be,
The bombs have left their open wounds for everyone to see,
The villages are flattened, no more shelter for the poor,
And the people on the sidelines are the casualties of war.

In a basement prison
For years they've tortured me,
All because I spoke my mind with simple honesty.
But free speech in this country means imprisonment and pain,
So in this hot, dark dungeon for God's sake I remain.

On a cross at Calvary,
A man hangs helplessly.
His face bowed down in anguish for the death that has to be.
And the crimes that he committed were the kindnesses he showed,
And the death he had to offer was the sacrifice we owed.

I'm the person on the poster, I'm the homeless refugee,
I'm your foreign neighbour in a far-off land.
And my troubles never touch you, from my illness you're set free,
And living is not easy no matter where you be...
But all I ask of you friend, is... spare a thought for me?

Alan Meacock

Meditation on Ploughed Earth

Ourselves, creatures of the soil,
At one with the soil, both once dust within the stars,
Ourselves to return whence we came, earth to earth,
Atoms recycled into soil, to grow again and again,
Soiled and sinful made new in God's unwasting creation.

The turned earth, to be broken down by rain and frost;
Our lives turned over by God, breaking through the hard crust,
      renewing friability.
Ourselves, a seed-bed for Christ the Word.
Rain, nourishment from God's Spirit,
In God's good time, a harvest, thirty fold, sixty fold,
      a hundred fold,
Unimaginable from the little seed,
Hard cased, yet bursting forth with God's tremendous energy,
Pulsating with new life,
Renewing this half - wrecked world.

Each of us a mini - resurrection,
Following the pattern of that mighty bursting forth from the
      mouldering grave,
Breaking the hard crust of human inhumanity,
God's weakness mightier than human strength,
Reconciling the world with its maker.
Ploughed earth, symbol of God in his world,
Help us to grow to his glory.

Rosamy Murphy

Greed

Champagnes and steaks
We like the taste
But some left over
It's only waste.

Foreign hols, a flashy car
A fancy sounding job
Unless you've got one of these
You're just a social slob.

A choice of clothes
A change of shoes
What shall I wear?
What will I use?

Credit cards or easy terms
Help buy the latest need
But is it really wanted
Or is it simply greed?

Videos and tele's
Hi-fi's, ansaphones;
These things are all around us
In our fully furnished homes.

But do we really need them
Those so called homely things
Or is it the social status
That having them will bring.

Simon Martin

Go Forth

When thy heart doth weary within thee,
    And the sorrows of man thou dost see,
Remember My Words of great Promise -
    Just to love and to watch over thee.

I place round thy shoulders a garland,
    That's entwined with the blossoms of Love;
Mine own Holy Spirit I bring thee
    In the form of a gentle white dove.

Be warmed by the glow of My Presence -
    Come and melt in the rays of My Peace;
Thy heart shall be lifted with gladness,
    And the Tempter's dark arrows will cease.

Go forth as the child I have made thee,
    With the flower of faith in thy hair;
Bring joy to the world as thou goest -
    Shed the Light of My Love everywhere.

Briony Lill

Sunset Reverie

Upon this summer evening fine
The sky is bathed in golden light.
From the sun which on its journey goes
And now is hidden from my sight.

And from my window I behold
A steeple pointing to the sky
Upon its tip a golden cross
Which maketh heaven to earth seem nigh.

While in the tower below the spire
Two little windows I can see,
Which seem unto my childish heart
As if the Lord is watching me.

And as I stand and contemplate
Upon the presence of the Lord
There comes to me a sense of peace
Which earthly joys cannot afford.

Oh! how I wish that all might know
This peace which only Christ can give
And that where'er the sun may shine
Men might unto his glory give.

Doris Cole

Of Regal Birth

Of regal birth, in earthy scene
Of stable and of straw;
The divine and the impossible
Now light the stable door,
And Mary cradles in her arms
The Father's living Word,
The story to belief is joy
To unbelief, absurd.

How can my finite human mind
Grapple with infinity
Appearing here in human form?
A thought of such immensity.
Heard I the flutter of an angel's wing
Or caught an echo of the song they sing
Then I too would be there with them
At the stable in Bethlehem
And joy would burst forth from my lips
As I cried out in my relief.
'Jesus, Saviour. Welcome Lord!
Help me in my unbelief!'

Gerald Gardiner

Shedding

In darkening world-grey days like this,
Crammed with uncertain answers from uncertain minds,
And stained with the wisdom of profanity,
Take me to your higher ground,
To your burning bush of Holiness
Where, unshoed and unworthy,
I can rest in your timeless permanence.

Shedding the dross of wanton rebellion,
And walking in the way of Holiness,
Let me enter your inner chambers of excellence
Holding the Holy hand of redemption.
And, entering your world of Alpha and Omega absolutes,
Your world of was and is and is to come,
Let the white light of sanctity
Penetrate my soul and break my indifference.

For although your Holiness frightens me
I know it is the only way,
The only truth,
The only life,
And that your word made flesh transcendence
Is perfect love that casts out fear.

Holy God, Holy Son, Holy Spirit, Holy One,
In darkening world - grey days like this,
Let me swim in your water of life,
Awe-soaked and dripping with eternity.

Coral Rumble

Requiem

When life's brief, crowded moment is no more,
The loved one gone.
What comfort can we find, or shoulder seek
To lean upon?

Can flight of busy hours suffice to fill
The quiet abode?
Can book and bell be all that's left of those
Who sleep in God?

He takes them home, who made them, sanctifies
The mourner's tears,
And leads us, hoping, on to heaven - beyond
The empty years.

Eddy Hughes

My Isaac?

I belong to a family that's always found voice,
And seized any occasion to sing and rejoice,
And most of the *get-to-gethers* we've had,
Were dominated by music - both good and *bad*.
For we were encouraged to lift up our voices,
And told *it's a sad heart that never rejoices.*

We were brought up on poetry - song - and the *ilk*,
It was Dad's contribution to go with Mum's milk,
And in our early years, there were concerts and things,
And all such celebrations where everyone sings,
For we were taught to make the most of our voices,
And remember the way that a glad heart rejoices.

I'm a lot older now, and without any doubt,
My poor vocal chords are fast wearing out,
And its no use clearing my throat, for I've found,
When I open my mouth - oft there comes not a sound,
So I listen instead to all other voices,
And reflect that a glad heart, indeed - still rejoices.

But miracles happen - though late in the day,
And I knew you will smile, when you read what I say,
For I feel like Sarah - when told she'd give birth,
And I want to *explode* like she did, with mirth,
For a *poet's* been born, and my heart can rejoice,
God's accepted my pen in lieu of my voice.

And what will my friends say to all this,
I'd better not ask them - for ignorance is bliss,
But I can imagine, when they knew I wrote verse,
My - her singing was bad - can her poetry be worse?
But bless them, I know each dear heart will rejoice,
That God uses my pen - same as He uses their voice.
Connie Webb

Maundy Thursday

Leave in the silence, believing
The words of the Christ are true.
Jesus said, 'Father forgive them
They know not what they do.'

Leave in the silence, believing
The words we are offered suffice,
Believe with a penitent thief
The promise of paradise.

Leave in the silence, believing
The work of the Saviour is done.
'Beloved, behold your mother.
Mary behold your son.'

Leave in the silence, believing
That the final burden is taken.
'My God, my God I am lost.
I am in darkness, forsaken.'

Leave in the darkness, believing
The Suffering Servant is slain.
Jesus cries out, 'I thirst.'
We need never be thirsty again.

Leave in the silence, believing
That, having received the wine
Jesus cried out, 'It is finished.'
Salvation is yours and mine.

Leave in the silence, believing
Though the darkness covers our land
Our Saviour commits His Spirit
Into His Father's Hand.
F G Whitelock

Jubilee

God is with us, God is with us!
How we marvel at His grace!
Vision of our Christian forebears
Grounded witness in this place;
Blended home with house of worship,
Private prayers with public praise -
God is with us, God is with us!
Rings out as in former days.

God is with us, God us with us!
Fabric of our Faith in song,
Cornerstone of our conviction
Sure as mellow keystone strong,
Stout as foursquare tower, rising,
Symbol of uplifted praise:
God is with us, God is with us!
Rings out as in former days.

God is with us, God is with us!
Unconfined by standing stone,
Present here, in glad assembly;
There where grief and pain strike home.
This our Lord Emmanuel's promise;
Thus, today we voice our praise,
God is with us, God is with us!
Rings out as in former days.

Anthony Harper

The Daily Battle

There are days when I scream,
clawing clouds from the sky,
when my body's in torment,
and my soul filled with ire.
When life seems all black
and not worth the fight,
through a gap in the clouds
comes a glimmer of light.
Pain is diminishing.
The drugs' work begin.
From the pit of despair
comes a murmur of hope.
Anguish, anger fall back,
clearing my mind,
to leave me serene,
and able to cope
with that day's battle,
once more in control,
Why me? is a question
I no longer ask,
knowing God in His firmament
cares about me.
I rest on His love,
for when I'm afraid,
He is my strength
carrying me through.
I trust in His mercy.
What else can I do?

Janis Priestley

Untitled

Sun dappled thoughts
In a cloud free sky
My feet hug the ground
While my soul flies high.
I'm surrounded by joy
For God loves me.
The Me that I am,
Not the me others see.
He gave me a gift,
A gift given in love,
To write from my heart
Of the lamb and the dove.
He gave us His Son
Who died on the cross
And said we should too
Put love before loss.
But still I can't write
Of all that He gives
His all is too great
Thank God Jesus lives!
Through Him we can feel
The greatness of God,
Through Him we can know
The true strength in His word.

Sarah Cope

Ponsonby Churchyard in June

So He giveth his beloved sleep

Here they laid him to his rest,
A man whose quiet life was blest
With faith and straight simplicity,
And knew a deep tranquillity.
Six sturdy shoulders to his bier,
His friends, his neighbours brought him here;
This hilltop with its spire and tall
Old trees, its graves, its haha wall;
And that which sunk in death's cold surf
They hid beneath this scented turf
Where bluebells droop as though to weep,
And the vetchling nods as though asleep,
And all the world is warm and bright
And shining in the summer light.

To make a cure for human ills,
Time, that great healer, often kills:
We struggle with life's woes and frets,
Death comes, Life goes: the world forgets.
Full many a fool might wish to be
Beneath that cold uncharted Sea,
Much nearer than the one that lies
Deep blue beneath midsummer skies
Not three miles westward! But the breeze
Which chides and mutters in the trees
Shall often murmur, in sad tones,
Its benedictions to his bones;
And I, who must with sorrow strive,
Can feel it good to be alive.

R G Head

The Robe

There lies upon the ground
A shabby thing
Poor cover for a king.
The soldiers diced for it
While earth was rent in two.
And high above
The man who owned it
Died, and dying gave a thief
Eternal life.
But down below a hostile
Unbelieving crowd
Just passes by
And goes into the night.

Ann Searle

The Hill of Life

If you may find the hill of life
Getting hard to climb,
Don't give in, but carry on,
You'll reach the top in time.

And when you have then, take a rest,
Look back across the years,
Remember all the fun you've had,
The laughter and the tears.

Think of the things
That you achieved,
When troubles came
The help that you received.

For God was there
At your right hand,
Ready to help
And understand.

He will be with you
To the end,
Your guide, your counsellor
And Friend.

Marie Pettitt

Some Verses from Psalm 104........
(Todays version from the 14th floor of an inner city tower block)

v.1-4

What can I thank you for, architects and planners?
You are bedecked with medals and certificates,
You cover yourselves with honour and prestige,
You have spread out the misery of the inner city like a desert waste,
And built your houses in the comfortable suburbs beyond,
You use the skyscrapers you've designed to feather your own nests,
And ride in expensive company cars.

v.5-8

You have set high rise buildings on insecure foundations,
So that they are in danger of collapse.
You build flyovers like a false ceiling above them,
And motorways like an ocean around them.
At your command they were constructed;
One word from you and they were built.
Tower blocks rose up, old homes were demolished,
All to the plans that you appointed.

v.23-24

Man goes forth to his work and to his labour until evening.
O architects and planners, how many are the problems you've created!
In foolishness and arrogance you've produced them all;
The cities are full of your monstrosities.

v.31-35
May the prestige of these architects and planners be quickly ended,
May they weep over the devastation they've caused.
I will curse these architects and planners as long as I live;
I will never have a good word to say of them.
May my complaints provoke them
For I'm in misery because of them.

Curse these architects, o my soul!
Curse these planners too!

Sheila Lloyd

Disciple

Walking in your shadow
content to let soft darkness
tease comfort to my soul.
Never dare to seek your face
in case
all those fears, through years
have names I know.
To touch heaven in your footstep's cup
but not walk side by side.
See the world in furtive glances.
Catch breath, bite lip
waiting for the blow.
Watching others in the sunrise of your smile
stand straight and grow.

Sue Hobson

Advent

Children waiting, watching, hoping, as the days go by.
Calendars with windows, door, to open and to try.
What will be their secret, waiting to be found?
A sparkling star up in the sky? A stable on the ground?

We too keep watching waiting when new babies soon are due.
To bring their pain and then their joy, a pleasure old but new.
A new life just beginning, to be nurtured from its birth.
To learn to seek and find that love that God knows each is worth.

Long ago another time of waiting anticipation.
Hoping for *Messiah* who would redeem the nation.
The promise was made man, Emmanuel had come.
But they did not see the signs, when this great deed was done!

God made man for all the sin found in this world so wide.
Unrecognised by his own kind, rejected, crucified!
But the light that shone in darkness could not be put to shame,
Through it each one could turn to God. Be truly born again.

Maggie Doré

Lenten Evensong

Hard February here: a crystalled earth
beneath a black cap sky,
thin laid-back moon.
Small sounds ring through this silence:
pleading bark of cold forgotten dog
the slam of door.

The church is warm with people,
starred with lights;
organ and voices revel in God's praise.
I do not sing: my head is lowered in prayer
for cold forgotten homeless,
human strays.

My eyes rest on a helpless fly
crawling painstakingly
along the aisle's red carpet
towards the cross.

The human church is cold and cruel,
no place with peace,
voices echo hunger, pain and fear;
but I believe, and hope and love,
crawl blindly on a perilled reach:
love on its way to penitence
creeps through a cobwebbed labyrinth.

Mary Atterbury

My Soul

My soul has reached to the skies
Soaked in the sun
Been refreshed by the rain
And cooled by the wind.
My soul has reached, yet not attained
The happiness it longs for.

My soul has reached out to others
Kissed by a lover
Been held in tender arms
And warmed by the laughter of friends.
My soul has reached, yet not attained
The company it longs for.

My soul has reached into myself
To find out who I am.
Been self-absorbed
And wrapped up in secret thoughts.
My soul has reached, yet not attained
The answers it longs for.

My soul has reached to the Lord
Basked in His love
Been washed clean of sin
And known the one true peace.

My soul has reached and understood and attained
What it was longing for.

My soul had been found by Him.

Sarah Threadkell

I Know There is a God

How can she see the petals of a rose,
Or look upon a new born babe in sweet repose,
Or watch the sparkling river as it flows,
And say there is no God.

How can she see the leaves upon a tree,
When Spring arrives in all it's ecstasy,
And bursting buds unfold, for all to see,
And say there is no God.

How can she see a blue summer sky,
With clouds like galleons drifting by,
And feel a gentle breeze, soft sigh,
And say there is no God.

How can she walk the quiet moors,
And see majestic granite tors,
The joys of being out of doors,
And say there is no God.

How can she see the sky at night,
In all it's splendour, glorious sight,
With myriads of stars and moon so bright,
And say there is no God.

What does she do, when sadness comes her way,
No wondrous peace, or hope, to help her through the day,
How glad I am, that I can say,
I know there is a God.

Christine Algar

Genesis

The yellow buds uplift their shoots,
The swelling leaves retinge the green;
Where once the unfelt life has been
Sunlight rejuvenates the roots.

Tread lightly here: let no foot-fall
Impede the thrusting daffodils,
For surging Youth all Nature fills
After the Winter's crusted pall.

Now spring to life all creatures, while
The dew-drops' glistening prismic tears
Are blown aside, and the earth appears
To have tasted deep the Heavenly phial.

Season of procreative strife
Battling with the Elements!
Springtime, with Easter, represents
Sleep transfigured into life.

Alfred John Winfield

Jesus

Before them all
You stood.
Less like a king
Should.

What throbbing pain
Of nail in palm
Amidst the anguish -
Calm.

Upon the wood
You hung.
While man his bitterness
Flung.

Your tender flesh
Nails tore.
So love outstretched yet
More.

O I would touch
That Hand!
For you, my Lord,
Understand.

Before them all
You stood.
As only my King
Should.

Mary A Foden

Manchester City Mirage

The sunlight dances on the water,
The ducks glide across the lake,
The swan swims straight and tall.
(And humans build a world of hate.)

Flat capped, silvered hair, men amble
Lovers smile, and walk hand in hand,
Children hide and seek in trees.
(And slowly we devastate the land.)

In this Manchester city mirage,
Civilised cornucopia,
I feel an uneasy peace.
(And so many are ruled by fear.)

> How can I be at peace
> When God's world is warring?
> How can I be at peace
> When God's world is dying?
> How can I be at peace
> When God's out there crying?

Those tears fall unnoticed by all,
As they enjoy the first warm spell,
Playing, walking, loving park.
(And the earth is turned into hell.)

David Hardman

The Way

Years ago I began a journey
on a straight, narrow, obstacle-free path.
Or so I thought.
After a time the path disappeared and
then became many paths in all directions.
It took a while to decide my way again.
Much of the time I didn't even try.
I didn't turn back, I knew what I sought wasn't there.
But I didn't know what I sought.

I chose a smooth and easy road,
wide and bending, with something hidden
round every corner.
Obstacles I could pass quite comfortably,
no need to venture from the safety of the road.
I didn't need to think, I could have travelled blindfold.
The road had become a routine... just a habit.
For me, it had no destination in sight.
A road that goes on forever, to nowhere.

If I look in the distance a light is shining,
between us many mountains and valleys,
sometimes a plateau, to rest and gather strength.
The direct route, well lit, an unmade track.
I must descend through the valleys and shout my thanks,
struggle up the mountains and sing for joy!
Without the depths would I know the heights?
I must keep my eyes on that constant, clear Light,
the Light that is Jesus, the Life, the Truth, *The Way*.

M Groves

Promises

There's a promise in each rainbow
shining high in the sky above,
That God will never flood our earth
because of his great love.
There's a promise in each snowdrop
as it blossoms in the snow,
That God created this whole world
and all we need to know.
There's a promise in each baby born
dependant, helpless, weak,
That Jesus died to save each one
tender, loving, meek.
There's a promise in each Christmas
when Jesus Christ was born,
That he would grow to show the way
to sinners so forlorn.
There's a promise in the rugged cross
so harsh and cruel and stark,
That everyone who trusts in God
will be led out of the dark.

But the greatest promise that I know
and one that's never broken,
Is the promise from our Heavenly Lord,
shown in his love unspoken.
That no matter how we've spent our lives,
if we truly do repent,
We will always be forgiven,
and to the Promised Land be sent.

Hilary Hutchinson

Ode to an Innocent
(dedicated to Pam, a young lady with Down's Syndrome.)

When I first saw you, I cried.
My hopes and dreams shattered, like broken glass.
Fear so real, so deep,
Feelings of shame, why me?
Imperfection - your beauty marred
Diagnosis - handicap.

Reaching, touching, holding
Warm against my breast
My tears of sorrow, falling, falling down upon your head.
I grieve for you my child, for what you might have been:
Hush now, be still!

Child of mine, so fragile,
Like a flower in full bloom,
Dependant, trusting, needing, innocent and true.
I was afraid to love you,
I felt so insecure
Emotions hurting, pain so sharp!
Tired and forlorn.

I rocked you gently in my arms,
You nestled close to me,
Our eyes met! Yours so clear, so bright,
They seemed to dance in the light
Then I knew love profound!
O sweet child, Joanna, mine,
Gift of God, serene.

Della Smithson

Christmas Thoughts

The sun in golden silence rose high above a hill
To give the world another day - and everywhere was still,
And everywhere was welcoming a new-created morn
As, in a distant stable, the Son of God was born.

Not everyone was ready for a gift of such great worth;
Not everyone was happy with the news of such a birth
And, as the sun again rose up, the crowd was calling *Kill*,
Pressing close upon a cross now placed upon that hill.

If we should choose to make our own the stable and the child
We have no choice but follow to the hill the cross defiled -
For those who seek the stable's joy and by the infant kneel
Must afterwards, if they're to rise, the cross' burden feel.

Derek Hurst

Within the Boundaries of Friendship

A smile, a wink, a knowing look
a silent embrace is all it took
to share my thoughts and deepest fears
my heart full of love, my eyes filled with tears.

A secret shared without a word
unspoken sympathy yet clearly heard;
Intuitive knowledge of my distress
healed in a moment by a gentle caress.

An expression of love that can't be defined
a tangible love of emotion and mind
a oneness, a closeness, a rare precious gift
the boundless love of true friendship.

Within the boundaries of friendship, Love's richness is revealed,
conceived of God and blessed by Him, it never is concealed.
Its loyalty, its freedom, its intimacy, its joy,
its honesty, integrity and selfless needs employ.

Such friendship warms the coldest heart
it brightens up the dullest day;
May friendship such as this my dear
be close to you I pray.

Caroline Rose

The Spirit Comes

I trudge on winter earth
unaware of stirrings below,
roots pushing down,
small promise of shoots and fruits,
as Earth's days' darkness recedes.
Dew settles,
nourishing these subterranean stirrings.
Spring rains swell torrents.
Deep in my heart ground is prepared,
space made for God.
       the Spirit comes
        who knows how?
Like a rushing torrent or a roaring wind
that shakes me to the foundations?
or like dew falling in the silence of the night?
Life conceived, slowly grows,
in fulness of time, will come to birth.
Fulness of life, fruits of His Spirit,
God's plan unfolds.

Tessa Spanton

Moses Reflects

All this was long ago and far away,
Yet fearfulness bites in every heart;
And I did fear, did fear great Pharaoh's rage,
Yet feared still more our Lord God's loving power;
A power that drove me on to leadership,
And made me strong to guide His chosen ones;
I, who had led no more than simple sheep,
And would most gladly lead them once again.
Sadly that simple life was not for me,
And I became the mouthpiece of the Lord;
The tool by which He forged His will for us.

So through the Red Sea wilderness we fled,
Pursued by Pharaoh and his mighty host.
We knew not how we went, but God the Lord
Did lead us by a cloud all through the day,
And by a shaft of fire when night did fall;
To safety led us through the sea of reeds,
And on into the wilderness of Shur.

Joe Whittaker

We All Have Our Prisons

We all have our prisons
Like Irina and Alexander
And countless others
Known only to God
In dank dripping pits
Of hollow suffering.
Can they be forgiven for believing
That God has gone?

We all have our prisons.
But we have no prisoners of conscience!
I can hear the pious cries.
But can't you see?
Can't you see
Shared slop buckets,
Caged confinement
And a fermenting of frustrated will?

We all have our prisons
Of guilt and hurt and anger
Which stink inside
Like the stench of canker
While we smile sweetly to those around.

We all have our prisons,
But Jesus comes
To set the captive free
In distant Russia,
In Holloway,
In you and me.

Peter Zimmermann

Time

Elusive, mysterious, time hastening goes on,
Like a river meandering, onward it flows.
The clocks tick the transient seconds away,
We cannot recall time, nor re-live the past day.

Time changes all nature by steady degrees,
Develops small seeds into tall, shady trees.
With time tiny babes become grown and matured,
In time sleeping life is revived and restored.

We waste time, misuse time, and time try to kill,
On happy occasions wish time could stand still.
For some time to have o'er again we have yearned,
But by time, from mistakes, true lessons are learned.

Time eases our heartache, time softens our pain,
Time teaches earth's losses bring heavenly gain.
Time character builds as it take us along,
Time offers fresh chances to rectify wrong.

Our time we should value, use wisely and well,
Seek the Lord, now's the time, holy scriptures tell.
His servants time brings to eternity's shore,
To dwell in His Kingdom, where time is no more.

Evelyn M Deakin

Seeing, Yet Not Seeing

When, on a Summer day, I saw
A briar that rosy garlands wore,
If they were flowers, but nothing more,
    Seeing, I did not see.

If, standing 'neath an open sky,
I watched the grey-lags riding high,
And was untouched by their wild cry,
    Seeing, I did not see.

If, when the fells with glory burn,
The glory of the withered fern,
For Nature's heart I do not yearn,
    Seeing, I do not see.

If I see children in sore needs,
Whose eyes for love and kindness plead,
And I pass by, and pay no heed,
    Seeing, I do not see.

When constellations slowly wheel,
And our Creator's power reveal,
If wondering awe I do not feel,
    Seeing, I do not see.

If, in the wood's deepest recess,
I walk in cloistered quietness,
unmoved by beauty's holiness,
    Seeing, I do not see.

Christ is the finest of our race;
And when I gaze into His face,
Unless I pray: *Grant me such grace,*
Seeing, I do not see.
Stanley Finch

Hope

Where is hope if hopelessness abounds?
It is in the sunrise parting the clouds,
And in the first drop of rain upon dry ground.

Hope is trust in sleep even though we find
This is a mystery not yet defined,
And we awake refreshed by morning light.

Hope is the last unbroken string
Still trembling on an ancient violin,
And in the first wild flower of Spring.

Hope is in all we know to be right,
To win over all the evil we fight,
And in deep joy true forgiveness brings.

Hope speaks of God's faith in humankind,
By the miracle birth of each new child,
And the treasure gift of shared parenthood.

Hope is in those values which are eternal,
In spiritual gifts unchangeable,
And in the selfless sacrament of friends.

For Hope is strong if coupled with Faith
Encircled together by Love's embrace,
And a three-fold blessing for life and death.

Marian Bullock

Stewards of the Lord's Supper

Chosen and elected by the Leader's Meeting,
A special duty in mind, a decision non-fleeting,
To prepare The Lord's Table for all who draw near,
A serious undertaking, not a few would fear.

Peter and John were sent to prepare
The Passover Feast, with their Lord to share,
A large Upper Room, well furnished and clean,
The Stewards reflecting, as they set the scene.

The fair linen cloth on the Table neat,
Washed, ironed, clean, for all who meet,
Its corners hang central, front, side and back,
Thoughts of the Upper Room, with care no lack.

The bread and wine prepared with care,
Mindful of the Last Supper and the Saviour there,
The bread and wine on silver arrayed,
Adding to the respect already displayed.

Quietly beckoning, with such grace,
The Lord's people are guided from their place,
With the Lord's invitation to all who are there,
No pressing, no fuss, just a loving care.

All who love The Lord Jesus are welcome at His Table,
Administered to all, kneel if you are able,
A mystery and blessing to all who repent,
Trusting, *In Remembrance of Me*, is the event.

The Stewards have prepared for His dear sake,
Putting at ease all who partake,
Years have past since the disciples were few,
The promise of Jesus is still ever new.
H Chilton

Legacy

'Confide ye aye in providence, for providence is kind,'
My mother used to say to me and oft comes to my mind.
'Be gentle to the old,' she said 'their race is nearly run,
And look with tenderness on them help them find the sun.'

'Care for the young,' she always said, 'they may have much to bear
They know not what may lie ahead, life's full of anxious care.'
Her words I now can hear so clear, 'Oh children, do not fight,
Love and laugh and aye play fair, and all things will come right.'

'Most freely give,' she always said. 'All you have, you must share.'
And many folks were greatly blessed by her most loving care.
O Courage, brother was a hymn, that was her guiding rod.
By example sweet, she placed my feet, firm on the path to God.

'Have faith and you'll win through,' she said.
And always proved this true
She left me greater wealth than gold!
This now I share with you!

Cathie Walton

The King's Highway

It is the same Road, even in our day,
Still straight and narrow is the King's Highway;
Nor can it be changed by human will
For it remains the Royal Highway still.

Turn not to the left nor to the right,
Look straight ahead and keep the Cross in sight;
The gradient may be steep, but never fear,
The Way is straight and the Direction clear.

And if our vision is obscured by night
Still He remains Our Friend and Guiding Light
Who, though invisible, is Our True Guide -
Forever with His Presence to abide

The Royal Highway still remains the same
And it is sacred, for it bears His Name;
It is the Way amid all fears and strife,
The straight and narrow Road which leads to Life.

Geoffrey Lund

I Am a Pearl Lord

I am a pearl Lord,
I am a pearl Lord,
I am a pearl Lord to your hands.
I dance with my heart's face to you,
I give all my love to you,
For you, O Lord,
For you, O Lord,
I set my heart's face to you.

Heather Connolly (6)

The Way Ahead

The past is behind, Lord,
many turnings I've missed.
Yet You remained faithful;
I've been greatly blessed.

Too often my own way
has caused us both pain,
but thank You for healing
and keeping me sane.

Be there at the crossroads -
I'll wait for direction;
still looking for guidance,
in need of protection.

You lead, and I'll follow
wherever You please -
that way You'll be Master
and I shall find peace.

Peter Swan

The Forgotten Friend

Friendship, inestimable friendship;
A prize sapling to be cultivated.
How sweet the fruits of such a labour.
The sentiment of shared experience,
The redeeming value of bared emotions.
I relish Your counsel and comfort.
When I am weak, You are strong;
And when You are weak, I am strong.
A burden for You wells within me.
How I grieve when we are distanced.

In the shadows of the woodland trail;
I sat all day and waited for You;
Yet, on passing You scarcely acknowledge me.
There was no embrace or token of affection;
You did not stop to express Your thoughts to me.
I had so much to tell, but You wouldn't listen;
- No time for idle conversation.
I longed to reassure You in Your uncertainty,
But You faltered and stumbled away with unease.
How I grieve when we are distanced.

Lord, I don't know You, that is really know You.
- I can't identify with divinity.
What then of God incarnate hung upon a tree?
Humble acceptance of humanity:
What of identification? - Oh Lord, this much,
You did first for me? Foreknew my vexations.
Forgive me for my insensitivity;
- For this dichotomy of loyalties.
Soften my heart and enable me to love You also.
Lord Jesus, be my friend.

Lisa Cornwell

If Jesus Came...

If Jesus came to visit our town
I'm sure He'd wear a worried frown.
His presence would make many consciences prick,
As thoughts flew to jealousies, underhand trick,
Foul acts, dirty language often used to express,
Lives totally empty, often meaningless.
Drink, drugs, illicit sex, too often take precedence,
The need for His Guidance is very much in evidence.
Mans' quest for power, so full of greed,
Each should look to this Traveller to satisfy all need.

If Jesus was to walk along our very road,
Decide to rest a while at our humble abode,
Would He feel welcome to sit at our table,
Sensing relationships ever-caring and stable?
Husband and wife to each other and to children
Showing true love abounding, again and again?
If not!... Why not?...
Let's invite Jesus to dwell in our heart,
We'll be assured of new strength to make a fresh start.
Every town, road and home will be ready for each trial,
And that worried frown would soon turn to a smile!

Betty Roe

Echoes

In some wild garden of my dreams
Where close the whispering poplar grows,
And o'er the ruined archway streams
The woodbine mingled with the rose,
I find a peace no words can tell,
A strange completeness to life's theme;
A healing touch, that seems to dwell
Within the garden of my dreams.

Within my garden, when the day
Is spent, and evening shadows fall,
A chilling wind begins to stray
Where Cypress trees rise dark and tall;
Another garden then I see,
Wrought in the moon's transforming beams -
That long ago Gethsemane, here,
In the garden of my dreams!

R A Ruddock

Lucy

'How did God make me, Mum?
What d'you think He did?'
My elbows deep in soapy suds,
I scrub the saucepan lid.

'How did God make me, Mum?
Where did He begin?'
My mouth is opened wide to speak,
The panic setting in.

'I know how God made me, Mum.'
'Oh yes dear, how was that?'
'First He made my head, Mum
And my ears came after that.

Stuck on my eyes and nose, Mum,
Made my body, and next
He put my arms and legs on,
With hands and feet that match.'

I turn back to kitchen sink
Light dawning on my face.
The questions that are simple
Are the hardest ones to face.

I know that God holds Lucy
In the palm of His hand,
Suffers her to come to Him,
While I lag far behind.

Jill Edwards

Hope

My wisteria is dead.
It cost me eight pounds fifty.
It was going to cover the fence,
Climb over the covered yard,
And go next door -
They like wisteria too.
A profusion of flowers,
Beautiful,
Mauvey-blue,
With a scent
To bring memories
Of a time
When one did climb
Round my window.
My wisteria will ramble no more!

But when hopes die,
Plans fail,
There is always tomorrow.

I have failed,
Wasted time and talents,
Killed my plans
And those of others
Dead.
But today
I can start afresh -
Jesus give new life,
New hope,
His plan for me is living.

And look -
There is a new shoot;
My wisteria is not dead.
Marjorie Evans

Soul Sounds

When my soul tunes in
to the sounds of God,
What do I hear?

I hear
a mighty rushing wind of Pentecostal power,
the Holy Spirit of God in full voice.

I hear
a still small voice in the calm that follows the wind.
For God does not always shout,
sometimes He whispers.

I hear Him
even when He has no real voice at all.
In His special silence,
the silence of eternity,
He communicates the peace which passes all understanding.

And I hear,
though it only comes with practice,
not just God's voice.
I hear the music of angelic choirs
echoing down the corridors which connect earth with heaven.

One more sound I hear.
It is a rhythmic sound that embraces both heaven and earth.
What is this sound?
Is is the heart beat,
the steady heart beat of God's love.

When my soul tunes in
to the sounds of God,
these are the things I hear.
Kenneth Whittaker

Harvest

The harvest is ripe,
But the field of grain bends
With every fresh wind that
The evil one sends.
The darkness is deep.
All around us men stray.
Like shepherdless sheep
They have all lost their way.

Like stars we must shine
That God's way may be know.
Our land has forgotten
The Lord she once owned.
Go and seek the lost sheep
Go and gather the grain.
Our neighbours,
Our nation,
For Jesus reclaim.

Linda Davis

In Quietness and Confidence Shall Be Your Strength

When the prophet fled, defeated, to the wilderness,
Burdened with self-pity, loneliness and fear,
Nothing in the mighty roar of earthquake, wind and fire
Served to reassure him that his God was near.

When the first disciples scattered from Gethsemane
Love and trust were overcome by dark despair;
Violence and murder threatened, God had veiled His face;
How could they perceive His hidden presence there?

And shall we, who follow in the steps of Christ today
Be permitted to escape such doubts as theirs?
Violence and greed still flourish, suffering millions starve,
And we dare to wonder if our Father cares.

Deep within his soul the prophet heard a still small voice,
Calling back to life a faith so nearly dead:
Later to Christ's followers came the promised Comforter,
Strengthening and empowering for the tasks ahead.

Though at times our spirit falters and our faith is dimmed,
Still God's quiet voice may speak within the heart;
Confidence restored, we dare commit ourselves anew,
And in His eternal purpose play our part.

Freda Head

Today is Mine

Today is mine,
I'll not waste it
In mourning the deeds of the past
The pleasure and pain
The loss or the gain
Oh, why do I hold them so fast?

Today is mine,
Not the Future
For God wisely marked it *Unknown*
From the *Top of the Hill*
All seems possible still
But the Future's in God's Hands Alone.

Today is mine,
I will use it
For *Now is the accepted time*,
The time to achieve
Love, suffer, believe,
This is the day and Today is Mine.

Joyce Faulkner

Seasons of Forgiveness

The fall is coming again.
I feel helpless to halt it.
And the compulsion, like addiction,
Is stronger than faith.

My confession hibernates in cold depression.
The shame is again a replay.
I've been here before, déjà vu,
And faith is locked in limbo.

Rebirth springs from confession,
And forgiveness brings new light,
A resurrection of confidence
To move forward in grace.

A harvest grows from gratitude
With sunshine and freedom.
An opportunity for re-creation
And the fruits of the spirit.

A cycle seasoned by His Love.

Richard Keen

Silvan

At night
I walked in the wood,
along a path lit by shafts of moon
silvering through the trees.
Shadows cast their nets on the grass:
in the play of the light
I saw strange shapes appear,
old men and mythic beasts.
Overhead, the trees clasped their fingers:
there was silence save for the hoot of an owl
or a rat scurrying home through the weeds.
No stranger, I blended with the trees, the grass, the leaves.
Ahead I saw a trail of light:
my eyes were pierced,
I blinked yet there it remained.
I saw the Master walk slowly in a train of white;
his eyes' sorrow, his hands clasped transfixed me.
'Where are you going?' I asked.
'I have come,
I have come into this darkness
to meet the man who is without.'
In his hand he carried a sword:
it shone and cut the shadows from the grass.
He looked at me,
and in his gaze I saw the Love
that had sung the Universe into life,
and I was still, at rest.

Robin Arnfield

Preacher

Can it be that this ragged man
mumbling through grey moustaches
from faded pages of the heavy earth-black
Bible has entranced these people?

Is it some secret Art or
unsuspected oratorical education?
I do not think so for he
has neither the intellect nor the guile

his only remarkable qualities are
a good and generous heart and
pockets rattling with sweets
for the children of the chapel

yet in this dreary meeting-house
the silence hums and faces glow
like those of children
playing in snow

unknown to them it was the cold
winter of this ragged soul
which birthed the warmth
which fires their hearts
long grieving over the
barrenness of his love
from which this
Spirit springs

Andrew Moll

Sign Language

He's engrossed in simultaneous translation.
The language I cannot understand -
Mouth forming words with no voice,
Hands a blur of movement.
But his face speaks!
None so deaf who cannot hear his spirited
Body language, spanning the silent world and mine.
Laughter and hope in his eyes,
Friendly, bridging the gulf
Between two cultures,
Two worlds.

Like the African
Who once put a sermon
From her language into mine -
Truths that I'd heard many times
So lived and sparkled in her eyes
They tongued her words with fire.
And when, as she spoke of Jesus' love,
Small muscles creased
Her dark skin into a smile -
We sat beyond time and place and race
Windowing heaven.

Christine Leonard

Challenge

Light of enlightenment
Piercing and sharp
Spreading and changing
Cleansing the dark
Revealing each other
Challenging need
Exposing your values
Making you heed
Painful and burning
Unable to pretend
Goaded to action
'Each man is your friend!

Raceless and ageless
Part of God's plan
Each one is important!'
I turned and I ran
Back to the safety
Of darkness and night
Weak and unchanging
God out of sight.

But light would not leave me
Cold in the dark
A catalyst for healing
It sent out its spark
And turned me towards it
Though uncertain and slow
'O God can you use me?
How can I know?'

'My son I will give you
To show you the way.
You are part of creation
Do not dismay.
Trust in my promise
Ageless and true.
Believe in my justice,
I even chose you.'

Judith Dye

Invitation

Lord of the earth and living things,
Lord of my life and all it brings,
When I'm singing take my praise,
When I'm drifting guide my ways.

Lord of sunshine, clouds and rain,
Lord of my moods of joy and pain,
When I'm soaring share my flight;
In the darkness, give me light.

Lord of smiles and Lord of frowns,
Lord of all my ups and downs;
Keep your loving hand on me,
For I need you constantly.

Valerie Pimperton

Gutter Theology

When a child dies - Where is God?
When someone is unemployed - Where is hope?
When marriages fall apart - Where is love?
When we experience hurt and grief - why is life?

Often we live life in the *gutters*,
The harsh places of our common experiences.
We find it hard to believe that God is there
But He Is!

The Christmas story is all about this very thing:
And getting involved in this planet earth as a creature in Christ,
God experiencing human hurt and pain,
God coming into the gutter of our lives
So that He might lift us above and beyond to the skies!
So can we know God - hope - love - and life.

P Longbottom

The Need of the Hour

If e'er there was a need for us
who are Gods children to be,
Really on fire for the Master,
we know its today...surely.

We see the days wax worse and worse,
-iniquity does abound,
It's we, who are the salt of the earth,
should reflect Christ's light around.

And what a need there is also,
For all Gods children to pray,
To o'ercome the tide of evil,
that's all 'round us in this day.

There's a great need for each of us,
as Christs foll'wers to live right,
Live our lives clean, pure and holy,
honest, truthful and upright.

As our Lord's return approaches,
we are made fully aware,
Satan is having his last fling
all around us everywhere.

The sign of the times indicate,
the Lord's comings almost nigh,
So, let's meet *The Need of the Hour,*
'fore we're raptured through the sky.

Jean Roberts

We Praise You Lord

We praise you Lord,
For the beauty of Summer,
The warmth of the sunshine,
The fresh morning dew.
Birds singing, butterflies dancing;
All these beautiful gifts from You.

We praise you Lord,
For the gift of friendship,
A shoulder to cry on,
And someone to care.
Kind thoughts, a letter, a phone call;
Just knowing someone is there.

We praise you Lord,
That you're all around us,
Knowing and seeing
All that we do.
Forgive us our weakness and failings;
And make us, Lord, more like You.

Penny Brooks

Heaven

I used to think that Heaven would be a meadow,
And I would run about on the green grass
Among buttercups, daisies, poppies.

I used to think that Heaven would be a vast concert hall,
Where I would thrill to the sound of the orchestra,
And sing in the celestial choir.

I used to think that Heaven would be the sun,
With Christ in the centre of that golden glow,
And I would be one of the prostrate, white robed worshippers.

I used to think that Heaven would be the immensity of space,
And I would be a tiny particle
Fitting like a jigsaw piece into my allotted place in that vast cosmic entity.

But now I think that Heaven will be the sea,
And I shall be a dolphin,
Leaping, then slipping through the soft silky water which slides over my
                                                                              skin,
And surfacing into shining phosphorescence.

Christine Woodward

A Poem for Good Friday

A Cross is raised
Upon a dark and lonely hill;
And fastened on its rough-hewn timbered arms
A Man is hanging still.
A Man who hangs in fullest agony and pain,
Who e'en today - by lesser men's misdeeds -
Is crucified each day again.

A Cross is raised
Upon a rough and rocky mound,
Yet, at its foot so level is the ground
That all may come,
Both rich and poor, both black and white,
And kneel before that Cross,
Accepted equal in His sight;

A Cross is raised,
And on that Cross with arms
Outstretched upon its beam,
The price is paid;
God, through His only son
Did thus the world redeem.

Trude Bedford

The Retired Gardener

My calloused fingers
    are stained brown and weathered like my face
through long contact with the earth
    and seasons paradoxical.
My life has spent itself
    in curious warfare with the elements
Coaxing from earth such things
    as give man's mind its peace;
such beauty as in this garden now,
    brought over many years by others to perfection.

Yet not quite perfection...
    round some corner I shall bend and pluck a weed
whilst old eyes focus gradually
    on a suckered rose,
Then slowly straightening up
    reflect how easy it would be
with time on hand
    to make a clearance here
Ah yes ... with time,
    time has run out both for this garden and for me.

Which sets me thinking
    about the future, and Heaven of my hope,
an extension of my work on earth
    where rather than experiment
I would grow the flowers folk looked for
    in the gardens of my prime
and in delighted recognition
    their remembered pain would fade
and being known
    - and knowing, would start at garden gate.

Kathleen Stevens

The Seekers

Lord of earth and sea and space,
God of all the human race!
Though we sail Your seas and fly
In the azure of Your sky,
Yet not we these marvels do,
All our knowledge comes from You.

You in Jesus lived as man,
There our happiness began;
Every life must yield to You,
Then we find our selfhood true.
Christ in us will live and grow,
When we choose to have it so.

As we bear our neighbours' load,
Helping them along the road,
We seek You with all our mind;
Who seeks thus shall ever find.
Universal Love our aim,
Be it ours that Love to claim!

D H Cooper

Go Forth with Faith

Go forth with faith, 'tis armour for the fight.
Step boldly thro' the dark, there'll always be some light.
With other souls so sorely tried, yet true,
Go forth with faith, God cares for them and you.

Go forth with faith, sometimes the answer seems
Much too obscure, but later meaning gleams.
Gold must be fired to rid of its dross.
Our faith proves right, when we look to the cross.

Go forth with faith, your road you may not know;
God guides your feet, your progress may be slow.
One day your life is joy, the next is pain.
He sent His son to save - your living's not in vain.

Mary L Ticehurst

Advent

I'm secure here
  rocked in the womb like darkness of the deep.
Velvet curtains in shades of purple
  hide me from your gaze.
I can feel your arms around me
  holding close my unformed being.
Then the warmth of nurturing gentles me
  to growth and light.
The curtains slowly part
  for shafts of light to pierce my soul
I draw back afraid
  as though touched
      by flying sparks of fire
And yet here also is your presence
      and your glory.
Come Lord Jesus let us dance together
      in darkness and in light
You in me and I in You
entwined in one anothers arms.

Maureen Bedford

His Presence

I find joy within my garden
And beauty all around,
The wonder of a spider's web,
Bright flowers bedeck the ground;
The music of the song bird
And children's laughter fills the air,
May's canopy of blossom -
A scene beyond compare.
The fragrance of the scented stock,
Nature's gift with me to share;
The mystery of an evening
When no one else is there.
But in the joy within my garden
I find God's presence everywhere.

Barbara E Higgins

Autumn Leaves

Autumn leaves, blown roughly from the branch, so long familiar place,
with others all around, now, by the intemperate wind dislodged and,
separating old acquaintances creates an unfamiliar loneliness.
With all resistance gone, helpless before each blast and brush,
purposeless, fading, bent, alone.
So seems the lot of man; life's vigour gone with weakened grasp. We too
become exposed, lonely, pointless; here a season then gone like Autumn
leaves.
But no! Man's spirit points to better things; the body just a temporal home
for that which God can quicken for eternity. In Christ renewal, resurrection
and the Hope of Glory fill our trusting Autumns with a glow surpassing
leafy gold.
Christ knew our loneliness, sorrow and dislodgement from familiar friends,
gross exposure to blast and brush - dead! Blown like an Autumn leaf
into a rocky hole, yet, He who made both life and leaf could not be
brushed aside but *Rose* and rising offers *Hope* to all who seek,
Next year new leaves will grow - the tree yet lives - and those whose life
is drawn from Christ shall find in Autumn's dispersal, *Hope*
and put on immortality.
Made in our Maker's image, though marred; rough blown by life and
chance, but, present fears, tears, dislodgements and separations are seen by
Him
(from Whom none is lost to sight as falling leaves may drift beyond our
gaze).
So let us see detachment from familiar things not as endings, lone and
pointless vanishing but as grace from Christ to give us better things,
Life that will not fade, fellowship that cannot wane
and purpose beyond all present expectations.
So, trust in Christ, disperse the gloomy autumnal forebodings and see in
Him the *Hope* of new eternal spring - in Him, once dead, who *Rose*
and *Lives for Evermore*.

D Parker

Genesis

The yellow buds uplift their shoots,
The swelling leaves retinge the green;
Where once the unfelt life has been
Sunlight rejuvenates the roots.

Tread lightly here: let no footfall
Impede the thrusting daffodils,
For surging Youth all Nature fills
After the Winter's crusted pall.

Now Spring to life all creatures, while
The dewdrops' glistening prismic tears
Are blown aside, and the earth appears
To have tasted deep the Heavenly phial.

Season of procreative strife
Battling with the Elements!
Springtime, with Easter, represents
Sleep transfigured into Life.

Alfred John Winfield